PROPHETIC POLITICS

CRITICAL INTERPRETATIONS OF THE REVOLUTIONARY IMPULSE

**Che Guevara · Jean-Paul Sartre ·
Herbert Marcuse · Frantz Fanon ·
Black Power · R. D. Laing**

Edited by
MAURICE CRANSTON

A TOUCHSTONE BOOK

PUBLISHED BY SIMON AND SCHUSTER

A Touchstone Book
Published by Simon and Schuster
Rockefeller Center, 630 Fifth Avenue
New York, New York 10020

First Touchstone paperback printing 1972

SBN 671-21408-X Touchstone paperback edition
Manufactured in the United States of America

CONTENTS

FOREWORD by Maurice Cranston, 7

CHE GUEVARA by Kenneth Minogue, 17
Senior Lecturer in Political Science
at the London School of Economics

JEAN-PAUL SARTRE by François Bondy, 51
Literary Editor of Weltwoche, *Zurich*

HERBERT MARCUSE by Maurice Cranston, 85
Professor of Political Science
at the University of London

FRANTZ FANON by Aristide R. Zolberg, 119
Professor of Political Science
at the University of Chicago

BLACK POWER by George Feaver, 139
Professor of Political Science
at Emory University, U.S.A.

R. D. LAING by David Martin, 179
Reader in Sociology at the
University of London

ACKNOWLEDGMENTS

Acknowledgments are due to the *Journal of Contemporary History*, which published an earlier version of Dr Bondy's essay on Sartre; and to *Encounter*, which published earlier versions of Professor Zolberg's essay on Fanon and Professor Cranston's essay on Marcuse.

FOREWORD

The essays in this book deal in turn with half a dozen leading theorists of the New Left. Some of these personalities, such as Sartre and Marcuse, are primarily intellectuals; others, notably Che Guevara, are primarily men of action; yet others, such as Frantz Fanon, have combined the writing of books with the fighting of guerrilla warfare; all would claim to uphold, in their different ways, the Marxist ideal of the unity of theory and practice.

In a recent series of paperback books, edited by Professor Frank Kermode, several of these same names are honoured as 'Modern Masters'. The word 'master' will not be found in the pages which follow, for the perspective from which this book is written is not only academic and cool, but sometimes sharply critical.

Even so, both the importance and the novelty of New Left thinking are acknowledged by all the present contributors. Clearly we are not dealing here with the type of thought that was characteristic of the Old Left, with its slavish adherence to the Party Line and tortuous defences of prescribed positions. The New Left boasts of its autonomy. It is independent. What is disappointing is that the rule of orthodoxy has given way to the tyranny of fashion, and the New Left is in danger of becoming yet another destructive ideology.

The Marxism of the New Left is based upon a new Marx. For the Marx these writers follow is not so much the economist, the later Marx, the author of *Das Kapital*, but rather Marx the sociologist, the author of the early philosophical manuscripts. Their Marx is, like themselves, a 'Hegelian' of sorts, a metaphysician, neither a positivist nor a scientific determinist. Their Marx is the philosopher of alienation.

This association of the New Left with the reformulation of Marxism may account in part for its appeal to intellectuals, for orthodox Marx-Leninism is open to devastating objections

7

which no educated person can easily overlook: the economic analysis contained in *Das Kapital* has been proved by events to be false. But even though Marx is discredited as an economist, the New Left gives him new life in the role of a philosopher, where his position is less easily assailed. For if their new Marx is a vulgarised Hegelian he can be defended by a vulgarised dialectical logic, according to which almost any contradiction can be given a rational coherence.

The new Marx is sometimes none other than the old Marx stood upon his head. For example Marx himself expected the working classes of advanced industrial society to become progressively more impoverished; he also expected them to enact the role of the universal revolutionary class, overthrowing the capitalist system and introducing socialism. The New Left does not entertain this hope. It despairs of any revolutionary action from the workers of the Western world, about whom Marcuse, in particular, has written with notable bitterness. In the eyes of the New Left, such workers are bourgeois.

But the New Left has found another proletariat, suggested to them in part by Mao, in part by Frantz Fanon. This new proletariat is composed—in the words of the title of Fanon's most famous book—of the *damnés de la terre*, the impoverished peasants and rural workers of the third world, the Negro inhabitants of the American ghettoes, together (in the view of some writers) with miscellaneous alienated drop-outs from the Western *bourgeoisie*. Colonial revolts are seen as signs of life in this new proletariat, despite the fact that most of the known participants in such revolts are far from being the *damnés de la terre*, but are sons of the middle-classes, like Castro and Che Guevara and Regis Debray and Frantz Fanon himself. But if the new proletariat is a myth, it is an important myth to those who want to believe that in turning their backs on the industrial working classes they are still Marxists, and perhaps even better Marxists than Marx himself.

Another element of novelty in New Left thinking, and again one which separates it sharply from traditional Marxist thought, is its glorification of violence. Marx himself believed that revolutionary violence might be inevitable, but he regretted it, and he had no sympathy with those insurrectionists and anarchists who relished the prospect of *la propagande par le fait*. Equally the orthodox Communists play down the role of violence. Communist *practice*, assuredly, involves violence – war, sabotage, torture, assassination and terror – in the pursuit of its aims. But as much as possible, Communist violence is veiled. Communist theory proclaims minimal force. It speaks of peace. Picasso's dove is the key symbol in Communist propaganda of the post-war years.

Earlier socialists who made a virtue of violence were dismissed as fascists. Such was the fate of Georges Sorel, despite the fact that Sorel used the word 'violence' in his own peculiar way, and never recommended the kind of violence that fascists used. Even Sartre, in his preface to Fanon's *Les Damnés de la terre*, makes a slighting reference to what he calls 'Sorel's fascist utterances' before going on to praise Fanon's opinions. But the impartial reader of both Sorel and Fanon is bound to ask: which is the more fascist? For Fanon's exaltation of violence is often closer to Mussolini's than to Sorel's. And what is no less remarkable is that Fanon's views on violence are echoed by almost all the luminaries of the New Left, including Sartre, Marcuse, Eldridge Cleaver, Stokely Carmichael and R. D. Laing.

Fanon gives several reasons for thinking that violence is good. 'Violence alone,' he writes, 'violence committed by the people, violence educated and organised by its leaders makes it possible for the masses to understand social truths and gives the key to them.'[1] On another page Fanon writes: 'At the level of individuals, violence is a cleansing force.'[2] Indeed, Fanon, who was a psychiatrist by profession, advocates the use of violence as a therapeutic device in the struggle against European colonialism: 'Violence frees the native from his inferiority complex and from his despair and inaction; it makes him fearless and restores his self respect.'[3]

[1] *The Wretched of the Earth*, trans. C. Farrington (Penguin Books, 1967.)
[2] *Ibid.*, p. 74.
[3] *Ibid.*, p. 74.

Fanon goes on to suggest that violence is politically advantageous as well: 'When the people have taken violent part in the national liberation they will allow no one to set themselves up as "liberators".... Illuminated by violence, the consciousness of the people rebels against any pacification. From now on the demagogues, the opportunists and the magicians have a difficult task.'[4]

Fanon lived long enough to be disappointed by the actual political results of anti-colonialist rebellion: when the Europeans were driven out, the indigenous 'demagogues', 'opportunists', and 'magicians' took over with ease. But Fanon's faith had already become the established dogma of the New Left. Sartre repeated it in his preface to Fanon's book: 'The native cures himself of colonial neurosis by thrusting out the settler through force of arms. When his rage boils over, he rediscovers his lost innocence and he comes to know himself in the act of creating himself ... to shoot down a European is to kill two birds with one stone, to destroy an oppressor and the man he oppresses at the same time....'[5]

Sartre, however, was a champion of violence in politics long before he read Fanon. He once said in a newspaper interview that the 'essential' problem for him was to overcome the idea that the Left ought not to answer violence with violence. Two of Sartre's best plays, *Les Mains sales* (1948) and *Le Diable et le Bon Dieu* (1951) are about this very subject; they argue that one cannot do good in politics unless one is willing to soil one's hands with violent deeds such as assassination and terrorism. The case Sartre presents is a simple one. Violence, he says, permeates all existing institutions and political relationships: therefore the only way to make any impact on them, or to introduce better ones, is to use violence. The idea of another war does not seem to disturb him. In 1966 he advocated in *Les Temps modernes* the use of 'counter-escalation' by the North against the South in Vietnam and begged Russia to intervene with missiles

4 *Ibid.*, p. 74.
5 *Ibid.*, pp. 18–19.

against American bases in the Far East, even at the risk of a third world war.

In his most substantial book of political and social theory, *Critique de la raison dialectique*, Sartre argues that all political societies rest on institutionalised terror. Indeed what he sets forth in that book is really a modernised version of Hobbes's social contract theory, according to which all men are naturally enemies (because of the existence of scarcity), and hence that men can be held together in societies only if they pledge to subordinate their private ends to the social end, and if that pledge is enforced by terror. Unlike Hobbes, however, Sartre hints that if scarcity were removed men might cease to be each other's enemies, and that in a world of socialist abundance a new and more pleasing species of man might emerge. Sartre takes care to emphasise that since scarcity has governed all history hitherto, it is impossible for us to conceive the nature of such a possible better world.

Herbert Marcuse, in some of his writings, is considerably more optimistic. But he, too, links his yearnings for Utopia with a demand for the kind of violence which he thinks will speed its coming. Marcuse has an even greater loathing than Sartre for the world of present-day reality. Sartre was for some twenty years a defender of the Soviet Union, because he thought of it as being somehow the champion of the working classes everywhere; but Marcuse has for long been critical of the Soviet Union, and he has no patience with the working classes of advanced industrial society. In what Marcuse calls the 'hell of the affluent society', he thinks the working classes are as much deceived and corrupted by material prosperity as everyone else. Even so, Marcuse agrees with Sartre that the institutions of existing societies rest on violence, and that violence is required to overthrow them. The 'violence used to uphold domination' is bad, but violence used against the established authorities is another matter: 'In terms of historical function, there is a difference between revolutionary and reactionary violence, between violence practised by the oppressed and the oppressors. In terms of ethics, both forms of violence are inhuman and evil

– but since when is history made in accordance with ethical standards?'[6]

Marcuse was one of several ideologues of the New Left who took part in the Conference on the Dialectics of Liberation held at the Round House in London in the summer of 1967. The theme of this conference was announced as 'the demystification of violence', an occult-sounding phrase which turned out to mean the clearing away of bourgeois inhibitions and apprehensions concerning violence. The most effective speaker at the conference was Stokely Carmichael (whose views are discussed in this book by Professor Feaver in the chapter on 'Black Power'). The argument of Carmichael's speech was that coloured people in America should reject the non-violence taught by Martin Luther King and adopt violence as a means to their 'liberation'. Carmichael saw the situation of the Negro population of the United States as being analogous in every way to that of the 'colonised' people in the Third World, and whereas Dr King had wanted to secure the rights of the coloured population in America by techniques based on Gandhi's *satyagraha*, Carmichael adopted the theory of Frantz Fanon, and called for a war of liberation of blacks against whites. This introduction of racialism carried the New Left yet another step further away from Marx.

One of the organisers of the Round House Conference was Dr R. D. Laing, a Scots psychiatrist who is regarded as a *guru* by many young readers, both undergraduate and 'underground'. Laing is by way of being a disciple of Sartre, and has adapted Sartre's existential psychoanalysis to therapeutic use in his clinic. Laing has also published (with Dr David Cooper) an abridged English translation of Sartre's later writings under the significant title of *Reason and Violence*. He also provides a link between the New Left and the ideology of the psychedelic hippie movement, since he has come forward publicly as a champion of mind-expanding drugs.

[6] *A Critique of Pure Tolerance* (Boston, Beacon Press, 1966), p. 103.

In many respects the New Left and the hippies are sharply at variance with one another: the hippies believe in dropping out, in withdrawing from society, whereas the New Left believes in changing society by revolutionary action. The hippies are pacifists, noisily dedicated to non-violence and love, which the New Left scorns; the hippies believe in intuitive wisdom aided by drugs, while the New Left believes in dialectical reason. But in spite of these seemingly insuperable differences, the New Left and the hippies are united by shared antipathies towards the bourgeoisie and the affluent society, towards the square and the old, and united also by certain fantasies about the innocence of man and the wickedness of rulers. It is these feelings, often diffuse and obscure, to which Laing gives voice; his book on *The Divided Self* develops a concept of alienation which, however far removed from Hegel and Marx, finds a sympathetic response in the contemporary young reader.

Dr David Martin suggests in his essay in this volume that Laing can be understood only in categories drawn from religion. Conceivably this is also true of others who are dealt with in these pages; I have called them 'theorists', but perhaps they should be seen as prophets and preachers, breathing fire and brimstone in the wilderness of an irreligious age.

MAURICE CRANSTON

CHE GUEVARA

Kenneth Minogue

CHE GUEVARA

Kenneth Minogue

I

Whoever seeks to disentangle a legend must begin by distinguishing the man himself from the stories woven around him. The simple facts of the life of Ernesto Guevara are that he was born in the Argentine in 1928, trained to become a doctor, led a roving life until he joined Fidel Castro in a guerrilla campaign which terminated successfully in the overthrow of the previous regime, spent several years as an international statesman by virtue of his position as one of the leaders of Cuba, and then led another guerrilla insurrection in Bolivia, where he was shot on October 9, 1967.

It is reported that, like many Argentines, Guevara peppered his conversation with 'Che', a fraternal ejaculation roughly equivalent to 'Mac' or 'buddy' or to '*hombre*' which Spaniards sometimes use in the same way. Consequently, Ernesto was nicknamed 'Che'. The actual birth of Che as a legend, long in gestation, can be accurately placed within a few days of Guevara landing with Fidel Castro's revolutionaries from the yacht *Granma*, in December, 1965. The disorganised guerrillas suddenly found themselves being shot at, and rushed to take cover. In his diary of the campaign, Guevara wrote:

> 'There, at my feet, was a knapsack full of medicine and a box of ammunition. I could not possibly carry both; they were too heavy. I picked up the box of ammunition, leaving the medicine, and started to cross the clearing, heading for the canefield.'

Two years later, the guerrillas descended from the Sierra Maestra in which they had toughened their wills and developed their ideas, and inherited Cuba from the ignominious collapse of the Batista regime. Che Guevara now held the rank of major – *commandante* – the highest rank in the revolutionary army. He had abandoned the doctoring of the wounded in favour of political and military leadership, and as one of the top leaders, he presided over the extremely numerous executions which entrenched the revolution in power.

On January 9, 1959, within a fortnight of the triumph, Guevara was made a Cuban citizen, and simultaneously legalised his name as Ernesto Che Guevara. When, as head of the National Bank, it was his duty to sign bank notes, he contented himself with writing 'Che'.

In the next few years he became a prominent spokesman for the Cuban regime, and took a crucial part in prising loose Cuba's economy from its previous close connection with the United States. Then he disappeared without explanation, and rumours circulated, including one that he had been secretly done away with. But he seems to have travelled for a time in Africa, and in late 1966 he turned up in Bolivia leading a band of armed guerrillas on the Cuban model. By the time he died, the man and the legend had fused together. To investigate Guevara, we must begin at the outermost periphery of the legend.

II

Che was a heroic guerrilla whose image (beret, beard, battle fatigue dress, cigar and gun) has decorated the walls of people – particularly students – all over the world. The Tricontinental Congress (purporting to stand for the underdeveloped peoples of South America, Asia and Africa) dedicated a year to him. In spite of the fact that he was a sworn enemy of Yankee imperialism, Hollywood made a large-scale film about him, and cast its current version of the matinée idol – Omar Sharif – to play him. And when at the end of the sixties, a New York stage production dedicated to violating every taboo the producer could imagine on a stage was mounted, it was given the simple title of 'Che'. Since Ernesto Guevara was no sexual athlete, this particular use of his name reveals the character of the legend very well indeed:

Che stood for opposition to everything objectionable in the established world of the middle twentieth century. Amongst a student population dedicated to a form of politics known as 'protest' the Che legend has become an all-purpose rallying cry. Nothing, one might imagine, could be more strikingly iconoclastic and individual than the hero of such a legend. One paradox of Che Guevara, however, is that he is an astonishingly typical figure, and perhaps the best explanation of the enormous range of his fame is that he has become the first Latin American legend built for export since the days of Simon Bolivar.

Let us consider first a typical example of the literature on Guevara: the extensive introduction written to the most accessible collection of Guevara's writings and speeches.[1] The book is called *Venceremos!* and the introduction was written by an American political scientist called John Gerassi. It begins with a report of a reaction to the news that Guevara was dead:

'. . . I was approached by a nineteen-year-old co-ed. She had tears in her eyes and a "Make Love Not War" button on her breast. "You don't really believe it, do you?" she asked. "I mean, he couldn't really be dead, could he?"'

This is a striking passage, because it gives the reader a clue to the type of writing he confronts.

Roman Catholicism has produced numberless popular 'lives of the saints' describing the deeds of and promoting an attitude towards a person who lived, by God's grace, an exemplary life. One of the features of such lives is an account of the attitude of others towards this person, and the function of this particular part of the story is to give a lead to the emotions of the reader. Where Gerassi is leading the reader is immediately made evident:

'. . . they (the people who grieved for him from afar) knew

[1] John Gerassi, ed., *Venceremos!: The Speeches and Writings of Ernesto Che Guevara* (London, 1968). In spite of its uncritical devotion to the legend, and some rather poor translation, this is a book of considerable charm and much the best collection of Guevara's utterances currently available. [It is available in the U. S. in a Clarion paperback edition, published by Simon and Schuster.]

enough to realise he was an idealist, a man who lived – and if the present news were correct, a man who died – for other people, for people he never met, for the poor, for the exploited, for the alienated, for those who feel, perhaps only instinctively, that they are merely tools in their society, tools of greedy and powerful men who do not really care about human beings.'[2]

The account of Che's life here flows easily into the familiar terminology of Che's rhetoric – the rhetoric of 'tools', 'greedy' and 'caring'.

As in all such lives, the character of the developed saint is, with the aid of anecdotes, projected back to childhood. 'Che made up for his poor health with sharpness and will-power. He roamed the town with a gang of urchins who clearly acknowledged his leadership, despite his physical frailty.' Again, we learn that Che's revolutionary effectiveness anticipated his maturity.

> 'The light and power workers [of Cordoba, in Argentina, where the Guevara family was living when Ernesto was 12] had gone on strike throughout the province, and the company was hiring strike breakers. Che organised his slingshot gang, and in one night smashed every single street light in the town.'[3]

His intellect, also, was precocious, and again we find that the emotions of others are used to guide the reader: 'My father,' a friend of Guevara's is quoted as saying, 'who was a doctor, was shocked to find Che reading Freud when he was only twelve.'[4] Or again, 'His aunt remembers that when she visited her sister, Che's mother, "We would listen to him gasping, studying, studying on the floor to ease his breathing, but he never complained. For him, it was a challenge."'[5]

It would be easy, but futile, to multiply these examples. Let us be content to note two other features of the life of a

---

[2] *Ibid.*, p. 23. [4] *Ibid.*, p. 27.
[3] *Ibid.*, p. 28. [5] *Ibid.*, p. 30.

saint, the prophetic utterance, and the tribute of enemies. We learn that when Che was in Mexico, he made his living being a tourist photographer in company with a man known as El Patojo. When Yankee tourists told them to go away, Che is quoted as saying: 'You may laugh now, but our day will come.'[6] The tribute of enemies comes from a remark said to have been made by Walter Sauer of the Export-Import bank, who had to negotiate with Che when the latter was Head of the Cuban National Bank: 'It was just like talking to another banker, except that the son of a bitch is an orthodox Marxist.'[7]

Considering its *genre*, Gerassi's life of Che is admirably traditional, and it is a useful guide to the kind of response provoked by the legend. 'Even Guevara's death, in the longer run,' (writes Professor Peter Worsley) 'has a symbolic positive value. Of course he failed, but so did Christ. Yet Christianity subsequently became quite important.'[8] It is clear that in finding comparisons for Che, nothing but the best will do. Further, the legend of Che is promoted and diffused quite spontaneously by foreign enthusiasts. But its source lies elsewhere. The cult of Che is a stable ingredient of internal Cuban propaganda, and has become an important element in Cuban foreign policy. Fidel, with the matchless fervour of a living politician praising a dead one, remarked that 'he left us his example! And Che's example will be a model for our people.'

This theme – the exemplary life of Che Guevara – is one incessantly repeated whenever Cuban politicians fall into the mood of exhortation, which, in view of the annually unful-filled targets for sugar production, has in recent years been frequent. 'Che' – said Fidel to his people when announcing the death of the hero –

'has become a model of what men should be, not only for

[6] *Ibid.*, p. 37.

[7] *Ibid.*, p. 42.

[8] 'Revolutionary Theory: Regis Debray and Che Guevara', in Leo Huberman and Paul Sweezy, *Regis Debray and the Latin American Revolution* (New York, 1968), p. 137.

our people but also for people everywhere in Latin America. Che carried to its highest expression revolutionary stoicism, the revolutionary spirit of sacrifice, revolutionary combativeness, the revolutionary's spirit of work.'[9]

These sentences are but a small part of a very great deal of rhetoric in exactly the same vein.

It is always difficult for an academic confronted with the simple faith of believers to keep a straight face; and since enough has been said to convey the flavour of the legend, we may immediately pass to the more interesting question of the extent to which Ernesto Guevara created Che, and the extent to which Che was forced upon him. It is, of course, part of the rhetoric of the saintly life to deny that the saint had anything to do with the creation of his own legend, and Gerassi tells us:

> 'Always erect, usually puffing on a Monte Cristo No. 4 cigar, Che tried to keep out of the limelight as much as possible, and only because Fidel insisted did he make public speeches.'[10]

As far as it goes, this does seem to correspond to the facts. What we have to deal with is, at the very least a genuine legend, not just a piece of engineered public relations. The phoney public relations is also there, however, in abundance.

As we shall see, it is a fundamental tenet of the revolutionary beliefs that, after the revolution, governments cease to be alien and oppressive things; the leaders are merely those who articulate the deepest feelings of the masses. In the consolidation of such notions, Cuban newspapers have frequently carried pictures of Che (or Fidel) at work in or near the cane fields.[11] The Cuban government has used the image of Che a great deal to serve this kind of propaganda for productivity. But in more subtle ways, Ernesto seems to have

[9] Fidel's introduction to the official version of the Bolivian Diary.
[10] Gerassi, *op cit.*, p. 41.
[11] See, for example, the commemorative issue of *Granma* (Havana), of October 12, 1969.

co-operated in giving the legend of Che a discreet push. He was responsible for the idea (pushed to ludicrous extremes in the Hollywood version of his life) that Che was the brains behind the revolution, whilst Fidel merely contributed the popular touch. Thus Ernesto once told Simone de Beauvoir (and no audience more receptive to such a confidence could be imagined) that he used to spend hours explaining a complex economic problem to Fidel, who would then successfully boil it down to half an hour on television the next day.[12]

But what sustains a legend is a life. Legends are essentially simple, relating to characters dominated by a single passion in whose service they overcome the obstacles of the world until the time comes to die. Che's passion was to make revolutions and to destroy oppressors. He led a hard, tough life and overcame many astonishing obstacles until the time came to meet the obstacle that would kill him. The reality is always more complex than such a legend, and infinitely more inaccessible. In the case of Guevara, we have available quite a large body of testimony, and above all his own writings and diaries.

III

Che was a Marxist in both his actions and his theories. His fame in this respect is such as to place him alongside Bernstein, Kautsky, Lenin, Rosa Luxemburg, Tito, Ho Chi Minh and Mao Tse-tung. Most of these leaders combined action with theory, but the theory is mostly subordinate to the action. Such was the case with Che.

What did his Marxism amount to? Here we need to observe the way in which Marxism itself has developed in the first century of its existence. Marxism in the nineteenth century claimed its following because it stood at the opposite pole from the attitudes of a professional revolutionary like Louis Blanqui, or a romantic anarchist like Mikhail Bakunin.

[12] Theodore Draper, *Castro's Revolution: Myths and Realities* (London, 1962), p. 91.

Marxism recognised the fact that a man cannot simply 'make a revolution'. It recognised this fact by asserting that a great deal of preparatory work must go into building up the proletarian organisation that will make the revolution. But it developed these 'practicalities' of the activity of making revolutions vastly further, till they had become elaborated into the celebrated philosophy of history known as historical materialism. Every society was seen as a ferment of 'contradictions' working themselves out by a steady process of which the human participants were often quite unaware.

Marx developed this line of thought so far that he reached the conclusion that no society would be transformed by revolution until its potentialities had all been developed. Capitalism, for example, would have to go through a number of stages until everything inherent in it had been worked out. And when that point had been reached, then revolution would come about as part of the natural process. The Protestant reformers and the merchants of northern Europe, for example, had overthrown feudal society quite effectively, in spite of the fact that they had no theory of revolutionary social transformation and their conscious thoughts had been focused on quite different preoccupations. Now this version of Marxism evidently leaves very little room for the conscious making of revolutions. Up to the point at which potentialities had been exhausted, revolution could only fail or generate a monstrosity; and beyond that point, the resistance to revolution was so feeble that it would in all probability be a quick and relatively painless affair.

Now this is the version of Marxism which made it the most important brand of socialism of its time. On the basis of it, nineteenth-century Marxists expected the revolution to come first in the most advanced industrial countries. It took a man as strong minded as Lenin to overthrow this theory. He had already significantly revised Marxism by developing a theory of imperialism to explain why capitalism was lasting longer than had been expected, and a theory of the party as the vanguard of the proletariat in order to build up the revolutionary organisation he thought was needed in Czarist Russia. In 1917 at the Finland Station, he instructed his followers to work directly for an immediate proletarian revolution, in spite of the fact that capitalism was very little developed in the Russia of the early twentieth century.

Lenin was the first really talented revisionist of Marxism, and after his time the history of Marxism is the history of men who showed the theory who was boss. Mao Tse-tung defied Stalin's orthodox advice and built a successful revolution amongst the peasants. And Fidel Castro, along with Che, made a revolution in Cuba which was so much based upon a practical sense of local conditions that it was only some years later, and under the pressure of economic need, that the revolution came to be approximately squared with Marxist theory.

By the 1960s, even Marxists themselves, long immured as they were in Stalinist scholasticism about 'correct' lines of thought, had come to recognise this. Marxism, they began to proclaim, was not a dogma but a method, and for its elucidation they turned to the romantic strain which is prominent in the very early writings and which also appears in some of the very late pieces. Here we find a Marx who is the moral critic of contemporary capitalist society, and who develops the notion of alienation to explain why it is that human life as we moderns know it is so impoverished. The new Marxism of the mid-twentieth century has thrown off the fashionable positivism that Marx had absorbed a century before; it no longer advances Marxism as superior because it is 'scientific' socialism. On the contrary, it throws to the fore the elements of Marxism which appeal to hope, and which inflame the will to make revolutions and bring the long awaited terminus to the horrors of capitalism. What remains of the old Marx is the idea that all the evils of the world compose a single system and that each man must fight for the revolution in whatever circumstances he may find himself. The Marxism of Che belongs to this latter kind.

Yet Che does seek to restore the original unity between the romantic and the 'scientific' elements of Marxism, and he does so with a simplicity that can only be regarded as savage, and impatient:

'There are truths so evident, so much a part of people's knowledge, that it is now useless to discuss them. One ought to be "marxist" with the same naturalness with which one is "newtonian" in physics or "pasteurian" in biology, considering that if facts determine new concepts, these new concepts will never divest themselves of that portion of truth possessed by the older concepts they have outdated. . . . The merit of Marx is that he suddenly produces a qualitative change in the history of social thought. He interprets history, understands its dynamics, predicts the future, but *in addition* [my italics] to predicting it (which would satisfy his scientific obligation), he expresses a revolutionary concept: the world must not only be interpreted, it must be transformed. Man ceases to be the slave and tool of his environment and converts himself into the architect of his own destiny. . . . We, practical revolutionaries, initiating our own struggle, simply fulfil laws foreseen by Marx the scientist.'[13]

Marxism is, then, taken entirely for granted. A fully conscious revolutionary, as Che understands him, has the same sort of awareness that he lives in a world full of exploitation as the average man has that stones fall down, not up. Revolutionary struggle is as natural to him as walking and speaking; and as he walks and speaks he makes discoveries about the world which happen to correspond to the 'laws' of Marxian ideology. It is here – in the area where theory is related to practice – that the Cuban revolution has made its major contribution to Marxism; it is here that a kind of individualist renaissance has followed the frozen middle ages of Stalinism. This is the contribution of Che, of Fidel, and it was brought to its fullest maturity in the writings of Regis Debray. It amounts to a new version of the supremacy of practice over theory. Latin America had long been equipped with orthodox Marxists, but they had not succeeded in making revolutions. On the other hand, people

---

[13] Gerassi, *op. cit.*, p. 184.

who *did* succeed in making revolutions did in the end turn
into orthodox Marxists. Such, at least, was the official view
of the Cuban movement, a view which (it has been plausibly
suggested)[14] has allowed Castro to support guerrilla movements in Latin America and to by-pass the existing communist parties whilst yet claiming, for the benefit of his
patron the Soviet Union, to be unimpeachably correct in
his line.

Che's Marxism, like everything else about him, is concrete
and practical. We hear little about historical epochs, and
very little analysis of class relations. We do hear a great deal
about the guerrilla. Developed into a theory, the guerrilla
generates the idea of the *foco*, the process of revolutionary
detonation by which a small band of guerrillas set up a centre
of attraction in the sierras and bring the capitalist or neo-
colonialist regime to its knees. It is essential to this theory,
certainly as developed by Debray, that the *foco* be regarded
as simultaneously military and political. No longer does the
commissar fight beside the soldier and guard the purity of
his doctrine; for the two figures are fused together by practice, and the guerrilla will learn in the fires of experience
what the urban communist has abstractly acquired from his
books.

This development of Marxism runs very quickly into a
problem which cannot but have struck anyone who has considered the history of Marxism. Marxism, we have seen, has
largely been developed by its heretics – the men who knew
when to throw aside the book and act on their own political
judgment. Further, this has now happened so often that (as
we have seen) it has received official recognition in the way
in which Marxism is now conceived. The whole notion of
orthodoxy, with its apparatus of 'correct' lines, has weakened
in the poly-centric communist world of the mid-twentieth
century. For those many, however, who wish to repair the
fractured unity of theory and practice every break induces a
desire to restore the unity. Consequently each change has

[14] D. Bruce Jacks, *Castro, The Kremlin, and Latin America* (Baltimore,
1969), p. 131.

been followed by a development of theory which purports to learn the lessons of the new experience.

The Russians, the Chinese, the Yugoslavs and the Cubans have all indulged in this exercise. Its logic is of course, inductive. It consists in transposing the most striking facts of the successful experience into abstract terms and generating theory from them. In this way, the successful landing of Castro and his guerrillas in Eastern Cuba, their difficult but successful struggle to survive, and their final overthrow of the Batista regime, turn into the theory of the *foco*; the fact that these men were revolutionaries whose acquaintance with Marxist theory was slim, and that they became increasingly sweeping in their ambition to remodel the social order, turns into the thesis that under guerrilla conditions the military and political struggles fuse together.

This kind of argument is, we have noted, inductive, and inductive argument has been subject to devastating criticism. Why, the critics ask, does the inductive reasoner select *this* set of facts, and out of this set of facts generate *this* set of general principles? For since logically all experiences are very complex, and capable of generating very large numbers of facts and principles, the inductive reasoner must have left out of his account of what he was doing the crucial principle which led him to select (rather than to discover) what he has found. The attempt to learn lessons from practice very frequently gets shipwrecked on this difficulty, and political and military history, no less than that of ideologies, is full of people learning the wrong lessons and being surprised by the reality they encounter.

The Cuban experience, then, began by rejecting a good deal of Marxism as being inappropriate to the special conditions of Latin America. There was good warrant in Marxism itself – indeed in Marx himself – for such cavalier treatment of established principles. But the ideological passion to realign theory with practice led to the production of a revised ideology which *would* be appropriate to Latin American conditions. Such a production is immediately subject to the same criticism as that on which it is itself based:

Need we assume that Latin America is homogeneous enough to be covered by such a general theory? Might it not be true that each region of Latin America, or even perhaps each separate country, might have its own particular conditions; might, in other words, require its own special theory? It would seem that Che, who worked hard to develop a Marxism appropriate to Latin America, did not carry his reasoning this far. But his fate has certainly provoked other Marxists to do so.

Here, to understand Che's Marxism, we need to consider the conditions of his Bolivian enterprise. Bolivia is a small and relatively underdeveloped country in the geographical heart of South America; and it seems that it was primarily this geo-political fact which made it attractive to Che as the detonator of the revolutionary liberation of the whole continent. It had a government which (like many in South America) called itself 'revolutionary', but was not so in any respect that Che would recognise; and it had an army which was small, ill-equipped, and had been savagely mauled back in the 1930s in a war with Paraguay, an even smaller and more primitive state. It had lots of jungle and plenty of peasants, and its economy depended upon tin, the miners of which commodity were frequently in a turbulent condition.

Anyone looking at these conditions with a fresh eye would light upon the tin miners as the evident beginning of a revolutionary movement in Bolivia. But it would seem that Che looked at Bolivia and saw only Cuba; looked at its wild and inhospitable countryside and saw the Sierra Maestra; looked at President Barrientos, and saw only the figure of Batista. What Che established in Bolivia was a carbon copy of what Fidel had done in Cuba. And since Che was, far more than Fidel, a theoretical animal, the conclusion is tempting that Che was the victim of his own theory. He seems to have believed that Cuba was *nothing else but* the first instance of a pattern that could be repeated in other parts of Latin America. He had, like so many figures in history, learned the lessons of experience – the wrong lessons. For what was missing in Bolivia was a thousand particular characteristics – the radical organisation in the cities, the feebleness of the Batista government, and perhaps above all the fact of leadership by the able, articulate, intuitive and entirely native Fidel.

Thinking in international terms, Che clearly thought that a revolution could be induced in Bolivia without a prominent Bolivian leader. No doubt he had to think this, since no serious candidate was available; but even beyond this inevitable deficiency, Che (and Fidel) exhibited an astonishing indifference to local Bolivian sensibilities. They failed to win over the peasants, they alienated the local communist party and they never managed to have more than a few effective Bolivians fighting amongst their picked Cuban veterans.[15]

In this respect, then, Che has run the whole gamut of experience available to a Marxist theoretician. He bucked the theory to make a revolution, reconstructed the theory to fit the revolution he had made, and then proceeded to demonstrate by his actions the inadequacy of his own theory. It is not an enviable odyssey and it is unlikely to be frequently repeated.

Yet the adventures of a man are not the same as the premises of an ideology. The accidents which often lead to fatal consequences in the world of action are a standing *ceteris paribus* clause for an ideology; and an adroit use of this clause will prevent any theory from being refuted. We must therefore qualify our conclusion in two ways: firstly, that Che's failure in Bolivia does not necessarily indicate that the theory of the *foco* must be discarded, for it may simply be the case that ill-luck and poor preparation led to that particular disaster. More importantly, the very failure itself has abundantly the heroic quality which Che often spoke about in his writings and speeches. Whilst the Bolivian episode did – to some extent – refute one part of Che's Marxism, it also illustrated another part, and one which, although of less interest to practical revolutionaries, is far more important in

[15] See particularly: Daniel James, *The Complete Bolivian Diaries of Che Guevara and other captured documents* (London, 1968). This book contains a long and penetrating introduction.

generating the legend. This part of Guevara's Marxism is his preoccupation with 'the new man'.

The most suitable text for illustrating this preoccupation is *Man and Socialism in Cuba*, perhaps the most famous pamphlet he ever wrote. It is here that Che states what may be vulgarly called the ideals of the movement: and the central ideal is the creation of the new man. This figure of the inevitable future is sketched out against the familiar Marxist account of twentieth-century life. Man suffers a kind of death, we learn, during the eight hours of his daily work, and even the artistic creations by which he might express the (presumed) anguish of his environmentally determined situation have been restricted by an ideological conditioning through which the monopoly capitalists prevent art from becoming (what Che thinks it must become if it is to be authentic) a 'weapon of denunciation and accusation'.[16]

Man is exploited, and consequently his moral stature is diminished; but this happens very largely without his awareness. His attention is focused (by the agents of the monopoly capitalists) upon the success of a Rockefeller, and diverted away from the unsavoury facts which made such a gigantic accumulation of wealth in the hands of one man possible. Since this is a rhetorical document, it would be unfair to press too hard upon its logical inadequacies. We need merely to note that Che has in full measure the belief common among men of his time that human beings are 'conditioned' by the environment in which they live, and that the adoption of revolutionary Marxism, although not inexplicable in terms of social conditions, is the one form of human behaviour in which man throws off his 'conditioning' and embraces freedom. Clearly this is an equivocation upon the notion of 'conditioning', for the conditioning that a man can throw off is no conditioning at all. What is evidently being used here is the commonsense distinction between proceeding thoughtlessly along the paths of habit on the one hand, and becoming more self-conscious and deliberate on the other. This latter is a casual distinction we commonly

[16] Gerassi, *op. cit.*, p. 547.

make; but as transposed into Marxist ideology, it is dressed in a different vocabulary and becomes a pseudo-science of social determination. What Che has to say about it is very little distinguished from the writings of any other exponent of Marxist beliefs; what does distinguish him is his intense interest in the other term of the contrast – the new man who will replace the spiritual cripple of today's capitalist world.

Often, the specification is extremely crude, since it derives from the easy device of inserting the word 'revolutionary' before moral words which are universally regarded as virtues. There are times when Che indulges in what is virtually self-parody, and exhorts us to engage in revolutionary struggle with revolutionary dedication towards revolutionary aims. In the end, the new man does not turn out to be very much more than a revolutionary paragon:

> 'We are seeking something new that will allow a perfect identification between the government and the community as a whole, adapted to the special conditions of the building of socialism and avoiding to the utmost the commonplace of bourgeois democracy transplanted to the society in formation ... the ultimate and most important revolutionary aspiration (is) to see man freed from alienation.'[17]

This freedom is specified in two main ways. The first is that the new man will be the possessor of a highly developed social consciousness. This means, presumably, that the category of the private will disappear from his thinking. It certainly means that the new man will hold the same beliefs about social reality which are already held by Che himself, along with the revolutionary vanguard. In other words, the distinction between agreeing with Che's Marxist interpretation of the world, and disagreeing with it, has been transposed into the distinction between being socially conscious and remaining 'conditioned' and unaware. The doctrine of social consciousness, in other words, is a vehicle of dogmatism by which the promotion of one particular

[17] *Ibid.*, p. 544.

interpretation of social life is being passed off as the only possible thought on the subject.

The new man, then, will be a dedicated communist. His second general characteristic is that he will be a dedicated worker towards the communal goal of building up the community. Since Che speaks for an 'underdeveloped' country, the actual content of the work of building up the community is, quite simply, economic self-sufficiency. What it would be beyond that is very little specified. But there is one part of the revolutionary work which is so powerful that it has infused the entire picture:

'Let me say, with the risk of appearing ridiculous, that the true revolutionary is guided by strong feelings of love. It is impossible to think of an authentic revolutionary without this quality. This is perhaps one of the great dramas of a leader; he must combine an impassioned spirit with a bold mind and make painful decisions without flinching. Our vanguard revolutionaries must idealize their love for the people, for the most hallowed causes, and make it one and indivisible. . . . They must struggle every day so that their love of living humanity is transformed into concrete deeds, into acts that will serve as an example, as a mobilizing factor.'[18]

Love is the master passion of the new man. It involves 'doing away with human pettiness'[19] and it will be both higher and more persistent than love found under contemporary conditions: 'There ought to be a spirit of sacrifice not reserved for heroic days only, but for every moment.'[20] Again: 'One ought always to be attentive to the human mass that surrounds one.'[21]

In praising the speech which has supplied these last quotations, Che's editor, Professor Gerassi, writes:

'. . . the author gently criticizes Cuba's communist youth for its dogmatism, dependence on official directives, lack

[18] *Ibid.*, p. 551.   [20] *Ibid.*, p. 311.
[19] *Ibid.*, p. 312.   [21] *Ibid.*

of inventiveness, lack of individuality – yes, Che was always fostering individualism – and continues with a beautiful, moving definition of what a communist youth ought to be.'[22]

Che's emphasis on the new man may, then, be taken initially as evidence of his attachment to individuality, but to an individuality of a new and more complete kind than exists now. If there is any part of Che's Marxism (by contrast with other features of his career) which is responsible for the legend, it is to be found here. Communism has often been associated with a soulless collectivity, a kind of endless *corvée* directed towards some remote and abstract goal. But here is a major exponent of communism outflanking the appeal of capitalism on its own individualist ground.

Significantly enough, perhaps, it is in passages like this that Che sounds most like an old-fashioned Christian preacher; and he may easily be presented as a man trying to fuse the best of the old moral ideals with the most complete attention to the social realities which religious exhortation in the past has often ignored. Nor can this theme in Che be dismissed as merely the attractive rhetoric of a man who was, after all, something of a poet. For in his enjoyment of power, Che showed a powerful and continuous hostility to the capitalist device of material incentives, because he believed that such incentives split people off from one another; he believed that they stood in the way of developing the only truly socialist motive for working harder – socialist emulation.

Yet before we take Che's devotion to individuality entirely at its face value, we must consider two important qualifications. The first arises immediately if we ask: What exactly does Che mean by 'individuality'? A man like John Stuart Mill, who in his essay *On Liberty* supplied the classic account of individuality, believed that each person has his own unique thoughts to think and lines of action to pursue; and in what Che would call a capitalist society, which Mill would call a liberal one, the laws and governing institutions should be so

[22] *Ibid.*, p. 9.

34

framed as to permit the greatest possible development of such resources of individuality. But we can hardly believe that Che is thinking anything remotely like this when we read:

> 'Thus we go forward. Fidel is at the head of the immense column – we are neither ashamed nor afraid to say so – followed by the best party cadres, and right after them, so close that their great strength is felt, come the people as a whole, a solid bulk of individualities moving toward a common aim; individuals who have achieved the awareness of what must be done; men who struggle to leave the domain of necessity and enter that of freedom.'[23]

These are individualities only in the sense that a tray of buns straight from the baker's oven contains a collection of individualities. Each is separate, but in all essential respects they are made up of the same materials, they have the same awareness of the same 'what must be done'. And if we pursue this line of thought further we shall find many occasions on which Che speaks exactly like an old-fashioned Stalinist agitator – or 'orientator' as Fidel guilefully renamed the function: he harangues the workers to produce more and to rise above their personal preoccupations in order to join in the common struggle. Indeed, this theme becomes at times so obtrusive that the inspiring notion of the 'new man' looks like nothing so much as a carrot to induce people to drive tractors more carefully, or to cease pining for luxuries like chewing gum and lipstick which are no longer imported from the United States.[24] And although it is perilous to extract a doctrine from writings which are fundamentally rhetorical, we must conclude that although Che makes use of the appeal of individualism, his view of the matter is consistently the one he expressed when he discussed revolutionary medicine:

> 'Individualism, in the form of the individual action of a

[23] *Ibid.* p. 552.
[24] See especially: *On Sacrifice and Dedication*, reprinted in Gerassi, p. 144.

person alone in a social milieu, must disappear in Cuba. In the future, individualism ought to be the efficient utilization of the whole individual for the absolute benefit of a collectivity.'[25]

There could be no better illustration than this of the way in which an ideological thinker appropriates an attractive term for propaganda purposes, and changes the meaning so that it means precisely the opposite of what once made it attractive.

The second qualification we must make to Che's individualism is closely related to the first. One of the most important differences between current capitalist society and the revolutionary society of the future is that the first has a government which must repress the people whilst the second has only leaders, or a vanguard, who are one in love and feeling with the people. The desire to eliminate politics from life, to create a community in which no one shall be rendered alien by his exercise of power, is as old as Rousseau and (in this century) as wide as the seven seas. It is by no means confined to Marxism, but it is a very powerful motor of that doctrine. To anyone who stands outside this current of thought, the aspiration can only seem delusory, the more so because it is precisely the leaders speaking most about love who have perpetrated some of the worst excesses of our time. The love which is supposed to unite Fidel and his people, for example, has had to emerge out of the early apparatus of televised executions and the constant hostility of some hundreds of thousands of Cubans who have preferred exile to the benefits of such a love.

We may go further: virtually all modern politics is an exercise of ventriloquism, in which the rulers speak *on behalf of* a populace which is most of the time necessarily mute. In the countries conventionally recognised as democratic – countries like Britain and America – this muteness is qualified by periodic elections, and by a fairly constant ferment of discussion and criticism. Nevertheless, it is of the nature of

[25] Gerassi, *op. cit.*, pp. 174-5.

authority that whoever holds it must in the end make a pronouncement which shall be accepted as the political decision of the populace involved. Now most ideologies are devices by which this ventriloquial act may be carried on with virtually no interference from the puppet whatever. A democratic government, having to face elections, must come to some terms with the political opinions of its working class. But a Marxist government does not have a working class: it has a proletariat, whose consciousness may (by the rules of the ideology) be objectively determined, and instead of a political problem the government is faced by a pseudo-educational one: how to make the people conscious of what it *must* be thinking (but actually may not be). A great deal of what Che has to say is part of this kind of ventriloquial performance. The justification of it – as given to a group of communist youth – goes as follows:

> 'If we – disoriented by the phenomenon of sectarianism – were unable to interpret the voice of the people, which is the wisest and most orienting voice of all; if we did not succeed in receiving the vibrations of the people and transforming them into concrete ideas, exact directives, then we were ill-equipped to issue those directives to the Union of Young Communists.'

In politics at least, a posture of humility often disguises arrogance; and those whom men wish to control they first drown in flattery. The 'concrete ideas' which the Cuban government articulates from the 'vibrations' of the people are indistinguishable from the practices of all the other countries in which Marxism has become the official creed. Here is Che discussing the central problem that arises from the pretence that there is no gap between a government and its people:

> 'And today . . . the workers consider the state as just one more boss, and they treat it as a boss. And since this [Che is referring to the new Cuba] is a state completely opposed to the State as Boss, we must establish long, fatiguing dialogues between the state and the workers, who although

they certainly will be convinced in the end, during this period, during this dialogue, have braked progress.'[26]

This is one more version of the Stalinist argument that no safeguards (such as an opposition) are needed in a communist society, because the only oppression is class oppression, and classes have been abolished. It is a Quixotic argument in the most literal sense, for no intelligent worker is going to be taken in by propaganda pictures of Che or Fidel out in the fields humping bags of sugar. And it is particularly Latins who will, once the excitement of the moment is past, treat with amusement such exhortations as that of Che to 'raise our voices and make Fidel's radio vibrate. From every Cuban mouth a single shout: "Cuba si, Yankees no! Cuba si, Yankees no!"' The political problem is that when the puppet does get restless, and the 'dialogue' fails, the ventriloquist generally resorts to clouting him.

IV

Our conclusion must be that although Che had a journalistic flair for the concrete detail, and although he was supremely sensitive to the intellectual and emotional atmosphere of his time, his Marxism is really very little distinguished from that of other Marxists. In the field of revolutionary guerrilla tactics, he will no doubt be remembered for a variety of devices and observations; he is the inventor, for example, of the 'beehive effect' whereby one of the leaders, 'an outstanding guerrilla fighter, jumps off to another region and repeats the chain of development of guerrilla warfare – subject, of course, to a central command.'[27] But in the field of theory he has contributed very little, which is not surprising, since he was a man who wrote gestures, postures, promises and exhortations, rather than arguments of any depth.

[26] Gerassi, op. cit., pp. 146–7.
[27] Gerassi, op. cit., p. 389. Che himself, of course, became an exponent of the beehive effect.

To probe more deeply into the Che legend, we may now move away from his Marxism in order to discover what significance there may be in the fact that he was a Latin American. But these two things are not easily separable, for there are two features of Marxism which nominate it immediately as a highly attractive outlook for politically-minded Latin Americans. They have lived for over a century in the economic (and sometimes political) shadow of their neighbour to the north. When Marx explains to his readers that capitalist life is a struggle between the exploiters and the exploited, any susceptible Latin American would have an immediate candidate for the role of exploiter: Yankee imperialism. When, for example, the rest of the world was finding President Kennedy the graceful embodiment of liberal virtues, Che was finding him 'so full of a profound conviction of a special destiny, full of a fascist conceit, full of arrogance and a concentrated anger because for the first time he was not able to fulfil his designs in America easily . . .'[28] Ideological theory and continental attitudes fitted as if they had been tailored for each other.

Again, Marxism supplies a satisfactory account of the predicament of 'underdevelopment' – a predicament painful to South Americans who, at the dawn of European industrialisation belonged to the European family of nations, possessing extensive literacy and a tradition of intellectual cultivation, yet failed to build up the sophisticated economies to be found in Europe and North America. For one of the advantages of the theory of imperialism, which Lenin slotted into Marxism, has been to interpret an 'underdeveloped' country or a colony, not as an area where development has not yet taken place, but rather where development has been prevented by the deliberate design of the imperialist powers. Thus Che talks about the 'struggle against the main culprits guilty of our backwardness'[29] and goes on to accuse the working classes of the developed countries of a certain com-

[28] Gerassi, *op. cit.*, p. 218.
[29] Gerassi, *op. cit.*, p. 532.

plicity in imperialist designs, a complicity which he notes, with a certain pride, has diminished their militancy. Marxism turns the conditions of economic and social life into a melodrama played out as a struggle between guilty and innocent parties; and it is this aspect of Marxism which makes it attractive to Che.

Finally, it allows Che to link together all his enemies into a single system:

> 'The "wars" between Costa Rica and Nicaragua; the separation of Panama from Colombia; the infamy committed against Ecuador in her dispute against Peru; the struggle between Paraguay and Bolivia; are but expressions of this gigantic battle between the great monopolistic powers of the world, a battle decided almost completely in favour of the North American monopolies after the Second World War.'[30]

Che hates the Yankee Imperialists, and he hates the local bourgeoisie (to which, of course, he belonged). The doctrine tells him that the latter is the agent of the former. 'Neo-colonialism', Che explains to us, 'developed first in South America, throughout an entire continent, and today it is beginning to make itself felt with increasing intensity in Africa and Asia.'[31] Che shares to some extent Mao's populist vision of the developed countries as 'the city' which is surrounded by a hungry and hostile countryside in the form of the underdeveloped countries. But even this vision succumbs to the one evident geopolitical fact on which he never wavers: that the hard core of imperialism is the United States.

But in making these comments we remain chained to the justifications generated by contemporary politics. If we step back a few paces we are enabled to contemplate Che in the context of South American history since the arrival of the conquistadors. A great deal of South American history is, in Salvador de Madariaga's striking phrase, 'heroics in pursuit

[30] Gerassi, *op. cit.*, p. 201.
[31] Gerassi, *op. cit.*, p. 530.

of chimeras'. It is a panorama of strong willed and ruthless personalities pursuing one *El Dorado* or another, right down into modern times. Put Che alongside Cortes, or Simon Bolivar, or any other of the vast number of similar men who operated on a smaller scale, and our judgment of him will quickly change. His ruthlessness in dealing with enemies and traitors pales into mercy itself by comparison with the exploits of these others. South America has long specialised in Liberators who brought little liberty; Che belongs to their number, and is in many respects an intelligent and moderate version of the type.

And even this judgment betrays an alien, Anglo-Saxon provenance; for Anglo-Saxons tend to think of politics as an activity whose end is to maintain and enforce a set of rules which will secure society against anarchy and dissolution in order that ordinary life may continue. By this standard, South American politics has not been a conspicuous success. But even the barest acquaintance with South American traditions will indicate that there are many moods in which the protagonists of politics are men playing a kind of desperate game, and testing the validity of their wills by bouncing their projects off the social realities they confront. South American politicians have by and large inherited a good deal of the conquering will of the first Europeans to subdue their continent, and of the missionary enthusiasm of the friars who came in their wake to establish a spiritual dominion. Seen in this context, Fidel's revolution and Che's Bolivian adventure look much less like the harbingers of a new dawn than the continuation of a longstanding practice.

In the rest of the world, Marxist parties have developed a powerful aversion to something called 'the cult of personality'; but in South America the same thing is called *caudillismo*, and it is difficult to imagine politics without it. Remember, in this context, part of a remark quoted earlier: 'Fidel is at the head of the immense column – we are neither ashamed nor afraid to say so – . . .' Sometimes within Che the Marxist is at war with the Spaniard; and it is only in Cuba that the adulation of the leader – inextinguishable

though such adulation seems to be in Marxist countries –
takes the form of using the term *jefe maximo*. Only God can be
higher than a maximum leader.

There is another aspect of the Spanish tradition which is
relevant to an understanding of Che: the passionate separ-
atism which has been one of its unfailing sources of vitality –
and disaster. In part this has been based upon local attachment. Wherever the British have settled abroad, they have
never broken into dissonant communities of Welsh, Scots,
Yorkshiremen (though the Irish, it may be noted, have done
a certain trade in the export of animosities). But although
they had a clear sense of belonging to the Spanish peoples,
colonists in South America have often been split into hostile
groups of Catalans, Basques, Andalusians and so on. This
separatist motive has often gone along with the expansiveness
of strong personalities.

The wars of liberation consisted, for long periods, of com-
peting chieftains trying to carve out principalities for themselves and much more preoccupied with destroying their
rivals than their enemies. In this context, Che's abandon-
ment of Cuba (which was, after all, not his country) to move
on to another area, in which he took good care to brook no
competition in the leadership, appears as the reflex behaviour
of any able, strong-willed Latin American leader. What the
exact relations were between Che and Fidel is very difficult
to discover, particularly at the present time when everyone
has a strong interest in lying about the matter. But we need
not emphasise the element of rivalry and hostility between
them very much in order to conclude that Cuba wasn't big
enough for both.

The cultural traditions of the Latin Americans may throw
further light upon the career of Che. Consider the following
passage, a very famous one, which Professor Gerassi uses as
the epigraph to *Venceremos*:

'Wherever death may surprise us, it will be welcome,
provided that this, our battle cry, reaches some receptive
ear, that another hand stretch out to take weapons, and
that the other men come forward to intone our funeral

dirge with the staccato of machine guns and new cries of battle and victory.'

This passage reminds us that Che was a poet, and it strikes a heroic note which is not often found in the emotionally arid stretches of Marxist writing. But compare it with another passage:

'From me you may expect my complete and unvarying submission. I shall arouse the world. But my one desire would be to stand beside the last tree, the last fighter, and die in silence. For me, my hour has come.'

This passage, along with much else about death, was written by Jose Marti, the celebrated Cuban patriot, who, after a long exile in the United States, landed on the coast of Eastern Cuba and was killed shortly afterwards, in the year 1895.[32] It illustrates the fact that, amongst the Spaniards of the new world, there is a tradition of political rhetoric of a heroic kind, and Che is squarely within that tradition. Further, it is hard not to suspect either that South America has been most tragically well supplied with enemies to provoke this kind of utterance, or alternatively that there is something inherently attractive to Latin Americans about the posture of struggle and death; so attractive, indeed, that circumstances will be bent a little towards the provision of such situations. Men vary in their talents; some are fit for peace, and some for war, and the warriors are sometimes as unsuitable for peace as the men of peace for war. It was the greatest of South American leaders, Bolivar, who proclaimed that his element was war.

But South America inherited not only the tradition of the conquistador but also that of the priest. If we return to the passage from Che which we have just quoted we shall find in a short space terms like 'funeral dirge', 'sacred cause of redeeming humanity', 'paying a part of sacrifice' and 'getting

[32] A convenient discussion of Marti and other elements throwing light on the Revolution will be found in: Ramon Eduardo Ruiz, *Cuba: The Making of a Revolution.*

ever closer to the new man', and (elsewhere) 'the holy idea
of production'. These are all fundamentally religious ideas.
It is clearly significant that the moment Che's emotional
temperature begins to rise, the most adequate vehicle of his
thoughts and feelings should be the religious idiom. He is, of
course, speaking to a population which has grown up in the
midst of Roman Catholic symbolism, but these are not the
calculated words of a man who merely stirs feelings the way
he might stir the contents of a pot: they express what he feels
himself at a level of experience just below rational discourse.
This is not to say that Che's Marxism is a religion, but merely
that it draws much of its strength from these strands of
feeling, and that their presence should be recognised by anyone who seeks to understand South American revolutionary
movements and their future.

V

So much for Che the Marxist and Che the Latin American.
What of Che the man? The only answer to this question is
his life story, and the difficulty of approaching so close is that
every life is equivocal. Any biography can record a failure or
a success, a tragedy or a comedy, according to the way it is
written. We may note, however, two themes which may be
detected in Che's writings and which seem also to emerge in
the pattern of his life. In both cases the themes may be
detected by a close attention to the metaphors that come
tumbling out of Che's (highly metaphorical) mind. And in
each case the metaphor is a common one amongst ideologists
but takes on a particular flavour from the way he uses it.

The first is the metaphor of the struggle. Che was the sort
of man for whom life can only be lived as a struggle; the
times of tranquil mediocrity are unbearable to him unless
conceived of as a form of preparation. What is the significance
of this preference? Clearly it is in part a matter of temperament. But if we press upon it we can discover its intellectual significance.

Imagine that the world is regarded – as it once was by the

Manichaeans and is now by the Marxists – as a struggle between a good and an evil force. Such a conception virtually removes the need of choosing a side; we shall obviously choose the good side in preference to the evil, just as Che chose to fight for justice and the people against the imperialism of the monopoly capitalists. Once this choice has been made – and it is a choice virtually determined by the terms in which it is posed – then everything else follows from it. Life ceases to be an endless movement from one situation of choice to another, a movement in which there is no clear criterion of the right and the wrong. Strictly speaking, all that remains are technical decisions about the right means to be used at any given time. To conceive of life in this way as a cosmic struggle is a way of choosing to give up choosing.

The second metaphor is that of going on a journey. Che manages to convert time into space, and the twenty-first century is not for him something that will happen on a calendar but a distant place towards which we may, with difficulty, approach. Here is a typical use of the image:

'The road is long and full of difficulties. At times the route strays off course, and it is necessary to retreat; at times a too rapid pace separates us from the masses, and on occasions the pace is slow and we feel upon our necks the breath of those who follow upon our heels. Our ambition as revolutionaries makes us try to move forward as far as possible, opening up the way before, but we know that we must be reinforced by the mass, while the mass will be able to advance more rapidly if we encourage it by our example.'[33]

In other contexts, the metaphor of a marching army has been a standby of totalitarian political thinking; and at bottom this element is present also in Che, but it is mixed with a good deal else. Talking to Cuban youth, for example, he uses an elaborate metaphor: '. . . The first days after leaving the bed one's gait is unsteady, until little by little a new sureness is attained. We are on that path.'[34]

[33] Gerassi, *op. cit.*, p. 543.
[34] Gerassi, *op. cit.*, p. 306.

The point here is that he has got his wires crossed, and the thought of walking has been enough to bring the metaphor of paths immediately to his mind. This otherwise banal trope takes on a new significance if we connect it with Che's life. From his earliest days, he was much given to travelling, and in his adolescence every vacation saw him mounted on his motor bike and off to explore: exploring first his native Argentina and when older taking the whole of South America for his province. He prejudiced his success in medical examinations by this kind of journeying, but was intelligent enough to pass. Instead of practising, he roamed. Guatemala, Mexico, Cuba, and then the world became stages of this ceaseless odyssey.

But unlike Ulysses, Che had no Ithaca to return to. He was in a very literal sense a man without a home. He himself agreed that he might be described as an adventurer, though one of a special kind. And it is perhaps in part a consequence of this homelessness that he was so strongly attached to a notion of the revolution as an international process. In his experience there would always be new countries in which the revolution would have to be made. But we may guess that if the revolution had succeeded all through the world a man of Che's romantic temperament would be ill at ease unless he had discovered some bureaucratic recidivism to fight.

The circumstances of the present world are such as to encourage the illusion that attachment to the revolution is an attachment to a once-and-for-all change in our political condition. But it is becoming more and more clear that the idea of revolution in the twentieth century is the political expression of a romantic temperament, and that it is a permanent struggle, against habit in oneself, tranquillity in one's surroundings and stability in one's government.

Che was, then, in the most literal sense of the words, a man who wanted to be 'going places'. His fame burst upon the world in the same decade as an international petrol company advertised its product by talking of the 'get up and go' people; and in the same decade youth came to be valued as it had not been valued since the first outburst of romanticism at the turn of the nineteenth century. With a slight change of attitude, a journey can become a pilgrimage, the religious version of the psychoanalytic tenet that the man who goes on a journey is often trying to leave his guilt behind and regain his innocence. The revolution is – and was to Che – an attempt to wipe clean the slate and to start all over again.

It is because he pushed this endeavour to heroic lengths that Che moved out of the class of South American *caudillos* and acquired the status of a saint. For although there was a powerful element of gambling and gaming in the attitudes of those dictatorial personalities who have swum across the political firmament of South America, there has also been a down-to-earth attachment to the benefits of power. Manuel Rodriguez, who attained an early death in the struggle for Chilean independence, replied to a prudent warning from Bernardo O'Higgins:

'I am one of those who believe that a republican government ought to be changed once every six months, or at most every year, and to bring this about we would do everything in our power. So deep-rooted in me is this conviction, that if I were Head of State and could find no one to lead a revolt against me, I would lead one myself.'[35]

This is the attitude of the pure revolutionary, and there have been plenty of them around, but they have not lasted very long. It is clearly not the attitude of Fidel Castro, who has evidenced no discomfiture at all in contemplating his tenure of power. But Che is not of this character.[36] After a number of years in which he held some of the very highest offices of the Cuban state, and travelled abroad as its official spokesman – both situations evidently very attractive to many men whose rhetoric would suggest the opposite – Che gave up the fruits of office. He took to the road, and set him-

[35] Stephen Clissold, *Bernardo O'Higgins and the Independence of Chile* (London, 1969), p. 170.

[36] See, on this and other points discussed: Andrew Sinclair, *Guevara* (London, 1970). This contains a useful account of Che's career, but it is very close to the Che legend, many of whose terms and assumptions Sinclair seems to take at face value.

self up as a guerrilla in remotest Bolivia. He died doing it. Exemplary lives are lived by men who follow their guiding passion without respect for power, comfort or life itself. The passion Che followed was less universal than that of many another saint. He was not a man for all seasons, but he has undoubtedly been the man for *this* season.

JEAN-PAUL SARTRE

François Bondy

JEAN-PAUL SARTRE

François Bondy

Three friends – two of his own generation and one younger – played an important part in awakening Jean-Paul Sartre's interest in politics; first Paul Nizan, the communist who had broken with the party after the Hitler-Stalin pact, and who even after his death in action in 1940 continued to be attacked by his ex-colleagues as a 'traitor' and 'police agent'; then Albert Camus, the militant member of the Resistance; and finally Maurice Merleau-Ponty, who for vital years was responsible for the political material in *Les Temps modernes*, the journal which he edited jointly with Sartre, and who once regarded the Soviet Union as the realisation of an historic hope which must therefore be judged otherwise than bourgeois states, but who later rejected this belief. Sartre has never been a communist and he has often taken the communists severely to task, particularly the French and on important occasions also the Russians. Nevertheless he has strongly attacked various intellectuals, including Marxists and contributors to his own journal, for criticizing the Communist Party too sharply.

Because he was never a member of that party, Sartre, unlike the avowed Stalinists, felt no special obligation to criticise the Soviet regime. In a reply to Daniel Martinet (not to be confused with Gilles Martinet, of the Parti Socialiste Unifié) Sartre wrote in *Les Temps modernes* of July 1950:

> As we were neither members of the party nor avowed sympathisers it was not our duty to write about Soviet labour camps; we were free to remain aloof from the quarrel over the nature of this system, provided no events of sociological significance had occurred.

Sartre never came completely to terms with the problem of how aloof to keep – was the Communist Party the only political expression of the proletariat or, as in 1956, a monstrosity, or both?[1]

Sartre was not an active member of the Resistance. He had founded a socialist society in Occupied Paris only to dissolve it again shortly afterwards in order not to endanger anyone. As he has never lacked any form of courage it was certainly because of external circumstances that he remained on the sidelines on this occasion. But it may have been because of his position on the sidelines that after 1945 he glorified and idealized the Resistance and was one of those who insisted on mercilessly tracking down anyone who had compromised himself; his attitude was thus unlike that of Albert Camus, who, fully committed in the Resistance, had signed appeals for mercy for collaborationist writers and journalists. The atmosphere of the Stalag in which Sartre was interned for almost a year, and which from Paris under German occupation, with its Resistance, he saw as a 'band of brothers', Sartre later recalled as an atmosphere of real freedom which he mourned and the like of which he had not experienced again. Until his newest complex investigations into the 'group welded together by oath', whose dual nature is both brotherhood and terror (in *La Critique de la raison dialectique*), freedom appears as identical with the militant conspiracy of a group and not with legal safeguards or with any democratic or liberal institutions, among which he singles out parliamentary elections as unimportant. The group which acts inwards and outwards, which faces the world and punishes its traitors appears, at least in this first volume of the *Critique*, as the only genuine antithesis to the 'practico-inert', the 'serial society' (of the type of the queue which forms at a bus-stop).

Sartre became convinced by Merleau-Ponty's *Humanisme*

[1] The following quotations clearly illustrate the contrast between Merleau-Ponty's changed point of view and Sartre's rigid attitude. Maurice Merleau-Ponty: 'The only correct attitude is to see communism in relative terms, as a fact which enjoys no privilege whatsoever.' Jean-Paul Sartre: 'To keep hope alive one must, in spite of all mistakes, horrors, and crimes, recognize the obvious superiority of the socialist camp.'

et terreur that in a revolutionary party, a revolutionary regime, opposition was objectively synonymous with treason. Merleau-Ponty had argued this, using the Bukharin trial as example, and the communists had not thanked him for doing so, because by this standard what they call treason can equally well be called merely opposition. Sartre in 1956 failed to approve of totalitarian rule exercised in the name of the 'project' of a revolution by which men determine their future, and even then more violently than unequivocally: this was when he condemned the suppression of the Hungarian popular rising by Russian armed force. For the rest he held and holds the view that a state run on revolutionary principles must be judged on the basis of its 'project' and its essential need to defend itself against a hostile world; that the logic of this state and its interests must always be borne in mind, whereas bourgeois states must be judged only by their errors, shortcomings, and crimes, all of which are in fact not accidental and curable but are the product of an original sin and can be removed only by a violent, purifying total revolution.

From Sartre's many political writings, speeches, interviews, appeals, leading articles, analyses, and from their many variations, apparent contradictions, self-refutations and changes, a relatively simple basic pattern never fails to emerge: social change must be comprehensive and revolutionary. It is the throwing-off of a bad system which is fundamentally at odds with the interests of the majority, like a foreign occupation. The party which embodies the principle of such a revolution – whether good or bad is irrelevant – may be criticised, but only by those who completely identify themselves with its purpose, its struggle and its road to power, although it must be understood that for this friendly and constructive criticism they need the distance which is gained from not belonging to any party.[2] Even without

[2] 'When a communist expresses the interests or feelings of the proletariat he speaks, rightly or wrongly, in the name of the proletariat. But you, Lefort, you, I fear are speaking *about* the working class.' From the polemic with Claude Lefort (a Marxist), *Les Temps modernes*, April 1953.

reference to Sartre's philosophy, which we shall here ignore as far as possible, this position may be described as 'existentialist'.

In relation to this basic structure certain striking changes, brought about by experience, are not of fundamental importance. This is true of Sartre's increasingly noticeable rejection of the European proletariat as the chosen instrument of the revolution and as the destroyer of the bourgeoisie, because this proletariat has itself fallen victim to bourgeois and apolitical tendencies. Simultaneously he turns towards the real 'damned of the earth', the masses in the colonial territories, have-nots who are expropriated even by their own people and who become the new proletariat, in the sense that they have nothing to lose but their chains. Sartre expected this total revolution of the *tiers monde* to lead to new, nobler forms of socialism, whose creative revolutionary impulses would then affect the European proletariat itself. In this context one thinks of Frantz Fanon, the doctor from Martinique who died young and who chose to become an Algerian on the side of the FLN; Fanon was influenced by Sartre, and Sartre himself was profoundly impressed both by Fanon's activity and by his theoretical attack on the whole of Europe and its spirit.

It was not until late in life that Sartre became politically conscious. He himself has often emphasised this fact, and this late development has been described with some self-irony in the second volume of the memoirs of Simone de Beauvoir, of whom the same is true. Sartre studied Husserl and Heidegger in Berlin when Hitler was already in power, and until the Munich Agreement was hardly aware of what Nazi rule meant. At the time he likened the ministry of Gaston Doumergue, which he characterised as a paternalist reactionary government, to that of the Third Reich.

It would be not only unkind but meaningless to blame Sartre for this remarkably long-preserved naïvety, this late awakening of political consciousness. It is more meaningful to note that political judgments as naïve as the comparison between Hitler and Doumergue also occur in Sartre's most political phase. When he said in 1954, after a visit to the Soviet Union, that he had there found 'complete freedom of criticism', when in the United States, which fascinated him to begin with, he registered only the breakdown of democratic institutions and the growth of 'prefascism',[3] when he noticed similarities between de Gaulle and Hitler, he was pronouncing judgments which belong to the period of his political commitment, his 'rebirth' as a Marxist. Such judgments were always supported by much new learning and passion without differing fundamentally from the amateur judgments of the period of 'guilty innocence'.

The early Sartre was well known, almost famous, even before the war, as a philosopher and writer, particularly through *La Nausée* and the collection of short stories *Le Mur*. In those days Paul Nizan – this at any rate is how Sartre presents the situation – relieved him of anxiety about politics. The communist fellow pupil at the Ecole Normale was his source of political knowledge and his conscience. We must see this early Sartre in retrospect as he presented himself in the preface to the new edition of Paul Nizan's *Eden Arabie*. We know that for Sartre, man in the non-authentic sphere is constituted by the way in which others see him, and by which he becomes petrified into a false, abstract essence. He is then *the* Jew, *the* bastard, *the* Negro, *the* thief,[4] and must accommodate himself to this role forced upon him from outside by making it his own, or else reject it simply in order to be a human being. However that may be, we can see the child *Poulou* only through the eyes of the sixty-year-old Sartre in *Les Mots*, and we cannot know Sartre's life until his middle

[3] In the leading article of *Les Temps modernes* (July 1953) on the execution of the Rosenbergs, Sartre expressed an indignation shared by most French intellectuals but went further than the rest in his demands for the cessation of all human contacts with these 'carriers of the plague', and by describing the execution not only, in agreement with unanimous French opinion, as evil, but as 'ritual murder'.

[4] 'What in fact is a thief? Nothing but a man whom honest people regard as such' (in the book on Genet).

years except for what he reveals to us with his backward glance – although one often suspects that this glance not merely recaptures 'time lost' but involuntarily adapts it to the requirements of the present.

The fact is that many of Sartre's political comments contribute nothing specific to the topic of 'Sartre and politics', and that nothing conclusive is gained from their precise enumeration. Frequently they merely confirm that Sartre's 'heart is in the right place' – that he was for the Resistance, against colonial wars, against de Gaulle's take-over, against the North Atlantic Treaty, etc., like so many other French intellectuals of the Left. Immediately after the war he had written as a supporter of European federalism and wanted to see French provincial nationalism replaced by a united Europe. As this particular article was not included in the collection of his writings in *Situations*, in which Sartre has brought together many pieces, including some outdated and vulnerable political articles, there may be some point in quoting more extensively from something which Sartre seems meanwhile to have simply forgotten, perhaps because it appeared in *Politique étrangère* (June 1949), a journal to which he made no other contribution:

> If we want French civilisation to survive, it must be fitted into the framework of a great European civilisation. Why? I have said that civilisation is the reflection on a shared situation. In Italy, in France, in Benelux, in Sweden, in Norway, in Germany, in Greece, in Austria, everywhere we find the same problems and the same dangers. . . . But this cultural policy has prospects only as elements of a policy which defends not only Europe's cultural autonomy vis-à-vis America and the Soviet Union, but also its political and economic autonomy, with the aim of making Europe a single force between the blocs, not a third bloc but an autonomous force which will refuse to allow itself to be torn to shreds between American optimism and Russian scientism.

In some of his attitudes Sartre was far ahead of events and of most politicians, in particular the communists. This is true of the wars in Indo-China and Algeria. There are other attitudes of his which seem like hasty, retrospective adaptations to communist changes of mind. For example, Sartre first described the Marshall Plan as a positive achievement which the people, 'contrary to the intentions of American imperialism', could turn into something advantageous later; after Stalin's veto on the adherence to it of Poland and Czechoslovakia, he attacked it as a particularly dangerous and vicious instrument of US imperialism. There are also instances in which one can speak neither of anticipation nor of adaptation; as in the unfinished, extravagant series of essays on an unsuccessful communist demonstration against General Ridgway and against the arrest of Jacques Duclos. When the Communist Party itself described its tactics as a mistake, the philosopher still sought to justify them and, as Herbert Lüthy has said, to prove that the party was never more the embodiment of the proletariat than at the moment when it was deserted by the proletariat.

In his immediate, skin-deep reaction to one or another event, Sartre is distinguishable from countless other French intellectuals only to the extent that in dailies and weeklies and in his journal *Les Temps modernes* he could always acquaint the public fully with his views. The militant atheism of *Les Temps modernes* and the Christian personalism of *Esprit* have not a single philosophic assumption in common; but politically the two moved along parallel lines for years in their hope for a new Left and in their anxiety never to have to oppose the communists, in spite of all criticism. The echo which Sartre's political opinions have found has little to do with their originality or their solid foundations[5] and has much to do with the fame which the philosopher, essayist, writer and playwright has acquired in other fields. His strongest political impact was made by two pieces of writing

[5] From among countless, often comic, examples of Sartre's use of 'Marxist' terminology as a substitute for proper analysis, I choose his definition of the Party of Lumumba: 'The MNC is the Congolese lower middle class in the process of discovering its class ideology' (*Situations V:* 'Colonialisme et Néocolonialisme').

which were not really political, the article 'Qu'est-ce que la littérature?' in which he says that the writer must be committed, and the play *Les Mains sales*, in which a typical child of the middle classes appears as the most radical, most extreme and totalitarian communist to whom the tactics of the party and its aims mean less than the continually repeated act of breaking with his own class.

Attitudes, opinions, a definition of the correct minimum distance vis-à-vis 'the Party' – it is curious how many static terms are required to paraphrase Sartre's political thought, although at first glance it seems characterised by the demand for revolutionary dynamism and unremitting militancy.[6]

Historically, as a happening, as the 'project' of a life, this political attitude becomes particularly evident in auto-

[6] 'For ten years the French intellectuals have discussed the big issues of the day so to speak in front of the looking-glass, in search less of facts and knowledge than of an attitude befitting their traditional role – of the "correct pose". The "testimony", the "personal document", reflecting almost without literary transposition the author's more or less profound reaction to his study of the press, the daily diary, published immediately, and journalism plain and simple, became the chosen form of writing for these thinkers whose militancy was such that it no longer allowed them to shape and hardly even to formulate their thoughts. In the post-war world one needed to make carefully balanced protests against tyranny in Spain and tyranny in Czechoslovakia, race discrimination in America and forced labour in the Soviet Union, executions in Persia and executions in Budapest, in order to preserve a clear conscience and one's own intellectual equilibrium which was constantly subjected to new threats. The intellect, which had been set up as the conscience of the world, became so problematic to itself that it could see all other problems only in relation to itself; in the end the only theme of the *littérature engagée* became itself and the *engagement* ended in solipsism. Jean-Paul Sartre above all, even in his polemical writing and in his plays, never dealt with any other subject and never had any other conversational partner than himself; among his followers a whole literature has grown up by intellectuals for intellectuals about "the intellectual", in which every ripple in the pond of this literary-political-philosophic debating club becomes a monument of the history of thought.' Herbert Lüthy, 'Frankreichs heimatlose Linke', in *Nach dem Untergang des Abendlandes* (Cologne, 1965).

biographical retrospect where Sartre takes stock and renders his account. In his piece on Paul Nizan he presents himself as typical of a generation which has become politically bankrupt; he recommends the young generation of today to take him as a warning example only and to remember instead the 'angry young man' Nizan, who had been a communist and whom the communists finally ostracised. Sartre had already named him in 'Qu'est-ce que la littérature?' at a time when Nizan's name could hardly be mentioned and when there could be as yet no thought of reprinting his forgotten works. With Paul Nizan's death Sartre lost a mentor and an alter ego. He was now compelled to fit the political dimension into his own life. He himself, says Sartre, had still shared in the euphoria of the Liberation:

> I recall that we had really acquired new and noble souls; so noble that I blush at the recollection even now. The nation allows nothing to be lost; it decided to entrust to us those insatiable and empty lagoons with which it could do nothing: the swallowing pains, the unsatisfied demands of those who had passed beyond, in short everything that cannot be restored. We were endowed with the merits of these martyrs. Alive, we were decorated for posthumous services. Killed so to speak on the field of battle: all the world whispered that we were the just; smilingly, lightly, or with sepulchral solemnity, we took this noble vacuity as a plenitude and hid our unparalleled elevation behind the simplicity of our behaviour. Apart from whisky, virtue was our chief diversion.[7]

But Paul Nizan, and Sartre later became clearly aware of this again, had always placed the class struggle at the centre. The communists, as Nizan had known them, had been 'unjust soldiers of justice'. But Sartre also tried to imagine what went on inside Nizan in the last month when he broke with the party, quarrelled with the world, and went to the front in order 'to fight against real men'.

He insisted on calling himself a communist. He reflected patiently: how could he correct the deviations without

[7] Preface to Paul Nizan's *Eden Arabie*; reprinted in *Situations IV*, p. 133.

succumbing to idealism? He kept diaries, he wrote a lot. But did he really believe that by himself he would be able to correct the relentless movement of these millions of men? A solitary communist is lost.[8]

According to Sartre, Nizan had learned that an individual in conflict with the party cannot have right on his side, even if in a particular case he is in the right; because the party is the movement of history itself. *Vae soli.* It is doubtful whether Nizan would have agreed with such an interpretation of the decision he took in 1939. Sartre's long essay on Maurice Merleau-Ponty appeared in a special number of *Les Temps modernes* devoted to the memory of the dead philosopher. It is the account of a close collaboration, of a ruined friendship which in the end was patched together again but never completely restored. When Merleau-Ponty, in *Les Aventures de la dialectique*, devoted a long chapter to what he called 'Sartre's ultra-bolshevism', Simone de Beauvoir replied in *Les Temps modernes* with her customary acidity. But Raymond Aron (whose original positions Merleau-Ponty had approached with this book), in an article entitled 'Les Mésaventures de la dialectique' (*Preuves*, No. 59, 1956), himself defended Sartre against Merleau-Ponty and demonstrated that there was no necessary connection between Sartre's philosophy and his controversial political attitudes. It was not possible to dismiss this philosophy, even in its political aspects, by criticising particular opinions. Sartre himself remained silent at the time. The heart-searching evident in his article on Merleau-Ponty revealed a human involvement that contrasts with simple political commitment.

For Sartre, in spite of all his 'progressivism', had now reached an age when the death of contemporaries with whom one is linked by ties of friendship and enmity leads one to remember the past, to draw up a balance sheet, because one suspects that one understands them better than younger people, with whom one may share ideas and aims but not memories and assumptions. Even before they became friends,

[8] *Ibid.*, p. 186.

from the Ecole Normale days onwards, Sartre felt a certain
spiritual affinity with Merleau-Ponty. 'We spoke the same
language,' he writes, 'the language of Husserl and Heidegger, because we belonged to the same school of thought.'
Only under the Occupation were personal ties established.
'In those days there was among the French a transparency
of the heart which was the reverse side of our common
hatred.'

After the war Merleau-Ponty was much more attracted by
communism than was Sartre. This is shown by his *Humanisme
et terreur*, in which Stalin's victory over his rivals, his victims, is
transformed into an act of justice. The two philosophers had
still been at one in their opposition to David Rousset, who
wanted to reveal the facts about the Russian forced labour
camps. They told him that the middle classes, the real
enemy, must not be given such satisfactions and that the
'workers of Billancourt must not be deprived of their hopes'.
Sartre decided to adopt Marxism, which he had up to that
time criticised as a form of Cartesianism, because he regarded it as the only intellectual weapon of historical progress and justice, whereas Merleau-Ponty examined this
Marxism more closely and critically, and read the works of
its interpreters, such as Max Weber and Karl Korsch. Sartre
regarded this as inopportune and was all the more anxious to
avoid a discussion of Marxism since in his own philosophical
sphere he still had reservations. Nevertheless Sartre managed
to present himself retrospectively as the more awake, more
open mind. He even claimed proudly that the readers of his
journal had followed him faithfully through thick and thin,
in all turns and changes, without noticing that this may have
been less a case of conscious agreement than of yielding to
the authority of an eminent mind and a famous man, a form
of subservience which he himself, had he been aware of it,
would have rejected as typically 'bourgeois'.

The human aspect of this article also leaves something to
be desired. When Sartre says of Merleau-Ponty that it was
their different 'rhythms of life' which in the long run could
not be reconciled, he is making things easy for himself. In the

same article he says about the Korean War: 'I have no doubt that the South Korean feudalists and the American imperialists have promoted this war. But I do not doubt either that it was begun by the North Koreans.'

Sartre says some worthwhile things about Merleau-Ponty's later works but finally he commits the same error of taste as in his interpretation of Baudelaire, whom he once proceeded to 'unmask' completely by examining not his poetry but his relationship to his mother. He maintains that for Merleau-Ponty childhood had been a paradise and that his mother's death had altered his whole relationship to the world and pushed him in a new philosophical direction. This line of argument reveals an inclination towards 'reductionism' which shows that Sartre was led to uncritical Marxism not only by political reflection but by a deeper instinct. In short, it says more about Sartre than about Merleau-Ponty; and somehow Sartre is conscious of this because he notes in himself an 'activist mania disguising many defeats'.

In Paul Nizan Sartre demonstrated the misery of isolation; in Albert Camus, in a controversy to which we shall come later, he detected the error of a flight from history. In Merleau-Ponty he detected quietism. This is curious because, particularly in *L'Express*, Merleau-Ponty repeatedly set out his political opinions. When Sartre and his friends launched the 'Manifesto of the 121' in support of conscientious objectors in Algeria, Merleau-Ponty collected many signatures, particularly of professors, for another important manifesto, more moderate in tone. He strongly supported the 'Pierre Mendès-France experiment'. These political writings are collected in his posthumous book *Signes*, and even if this phase of Merleau-Ponty's political thought did not appeal to Sartre, it does not permit him to dispose of the philosopher as a 'quietist'.

Nizan had led Sartre to the threshold of communism, and Camus, among others, had led him to the threshold of Resistance activity. It was Merleau-Ponty who made him realise that each communist regime had its own characteristics and should not be judged by the same criteria of individual progress or individual freedom as the pre-revolutionary states burdened by their historical past. Nizan and Merleau-Ponty made Sartre politically conscious. But when they went beyond the point where Sartre could follow them they lost all political standing in his eyes. He himself held fast to the perceptions they had imparted, for which he remained grateful and which he did not abandon. In that sense, looking back on the years 1960 and 1961 becomes for him an act of self-affirmation.

Sartre's attitude towards communism amounts to this: never to judge from outside nor to allow the discipline of belonging to interfere with judgment. If this seems paradoxical and strictly impossible, it is for Sartre a question of persevering in this paradox, in this impossibility. From instance to instance this attitude may seem irrational and inconsistent; but it can be shown – Sartre is convinced of this – that anyone who adopts a different attitude will find himself in a profound mess. Anyone who criticises the party from outside, without identifying himself with its power, its aims, is – whether he wants to be or not – an anti-communist. And 'An anti-communist is a cur, I'll stick to that.'

Sartre's famous reply to Camus came ten years before the article on Merleau-Ponty. It ended with the words: 'I hope that our silence will allow this controversy to be forgotten.' But this certainly did not happen. It is easy to show – Raymond Aron and Herbert Lüthy have done so effectively – that in the dispute between Camus and Sartre abstractions are marshalled against each other, and that anxiety about the correct attitude of the intellectual seems greater than curiosity about the truth. As a controversy among ideologists, this dispute typifies the spirit of Saint-Germain des Près and now seems incomprehensible anywhere except on the Left Bank or at the most in France generally. But whether legitimate or not, the universality of this great clash over politics, morals, and historical consciousness, over the relationship of revolution and freedom, has been confirmed by the echo which it found from Tokyo to Rio de Janeiro. The dispute has been immortalized in the collected works of the two authors. Camus's letter – a reply addressed to Sartre to a criticism by Francis Jeanson of his book *L'homme révolté*, which had wounded him – is found in the second volume of his collected works in the Pléiade edition. Sartre's reply is in *Situations IV*.

When the review of his book appeared, Camus protested against the whole trend of *Les Temps modernes*, with which he did not wish to be identified. A challenge on questions of principle was, however, unhappily mixed up with the attack by a sensitive author on his reviewer. But after reading the two pieces, and Sartre's article written after the Russian intervention in Hungary, *Le fantôme de Staline*, it appears that Sartre has come to agree with Camus; because he now judges a political event within the communist system by the same moral criteria as revolt and oppression in the West and in the colonies.

The theory that the Communist Party, whatever its mistakes, is always the representative of the proletariat 'against which one cannot be right in the end', is corrected in a conversation quoted by the author of *Les Existentialistes et la politique*, Michel Antoine Brunier:[9]

> Is it possible to conceive of democracy within the party except when the times are revolutionary? A party in non-revolutionary times is a party of expectation. It must mobilise as well as demobilise. This is the problem of the Church as soon as the kingdom of God is no longer for to-morrow. The party of expectation can be judged only by its actions: it is not legitimate as such. It is legitimate only if it acts as it should. Therefore one cannot imagine any *true* representatives of the proletariat in a state of expectation or under a dictatorship of the Stalinist type. This thought on the concept of legitimacy is missing in *Les Communistes et la paix*.

This statement represents the strongest self-criticism of everything that Sartre wrote between 1950 and 1956 on the Communist Party as the only legitimate representative of the

[9] Published in November 1966, collection *Idées* Gallimard, p. 95.

proletariat. Not only is this concept 'missing' from the series of articles referred to: their entire content represents the exact opposite. After the Hungarian rising Sartre recognised the existence of a gap between the proletariat and its political 'representative'. 'In spite of everything the Rakosi regime stood for socialisation. Only it did so badly, and this is worse than not to do so at all.'[10]

Camus thought that the dignity of the 'homme révolté' must come into conflict with totalitarian, petrified revolution, an idea soon proved correct by the workers' risings and popular movements in eastern Europe. But at the time, even in the few months before October 1956, Sartre in principle was moving ever closer to Stalinism, at a time when many intellectuals who otherwise had much in common with him were moving in the opposite direction. Hence his 'replies' to Claude Lefort and Pierre Naville, his attack on Pierre Hervé, and his identification of Stalin, communism and the proletariat in Les Communistes et la paix. If at any time Sartre went through a special political development not typical of a whole group, it was from 1951 to October 1956.

In his reply to Camus, Sartre had expressed his hope for certain reforms within the communist bloc and had written: 'One must be able to bear a great deal in order to change a little.' To apply the same reformist wisdom to a bourgeois world still in need of revolution is unthinkable for Sartre. For Albert Camus totalitarianism was a greater evil than a capitalist world. In 1956 Sartre saw in Hungary the kind of revolution of which he had dreamed: a contact between intellectual circles and broadly based mass movements, an activism shared by intellectuals and workers, revolution as an explosion of spontaneity. Reading Sartre's reply to Camus after all these years, we are struck by the mixture of dishonesty and bubbling verve with which Sartre indulges in misquotation in order to ridicule his opponents with the quick wit of the experienced playwright. In 1956 history provided striking and tragic confirmation of Camus' point of view.

[10] 'Le fantôme de Staline', Les Temps modernes, 1956–7.

What is the situation now? In a communist world in which the rulers cannot be overthrown by revolution or removed from outside, the problem of reform takes on a different character from that of ten years earlier; as a result of the crisis in the various communist regimes, the gropings for reform can no longer be completely suppressed. The views held by Sartre in 1952 have at least become debatable today. But more important than the question of who was right in the end or how being right became a relative issue as the result of historical developments, is the observation that both Camus and Sartre acted as intellectual ferment in the East and continue to do so, that their ideas are part of the re-awakening which is globally described as revisionism. Sartre as philosopher has always stood for an open, intellectually alive Marxism against inquisitorial doctrinalism. In Stalin's day this seemed a private refinement and what was of particular importance then was Sartre's strong resistance to any form of opposition to the communist bloc. His justification of the North Korean attack was the occasion of his break with Merleau-Ponty.

In *Les Existentialistes et la politique*, an uncritically devout book which is nevertheless very useful as a collection of quotations, Brunier documents the 'Polish phase' of *Les Temps modernes* between 1957 and 1958: there was a special number on Poland, and this was also the period of Sartre's long essay for a Polish journal which, as *Questions de méthode*, became the first piece in the *Critique de la raison dialectique*. This was the period in which Sartre spent much of his time in Italy and about which Simone de Beauvoir has written extensively in the third volume of her memoirs, *La Force des choses*. This was also the period in which Sartre became friendly with Palmiro Togliatti. To the intense anger of French communists, Sartre said in February 1963: 'If I were an Italian I would join the Italian Communist Party.'[11]

[11] There is a sad comment on this in an almost conciliatory article in a French communist periodical: 'He continues to sulk with the French party. He clearly finds it easier to reach an understanding with communists elsewhere. . . . There is in Sartre a desire for recognition which

The intellectual flexibility, the conciliatory and tolerant tone of the theoretical disputes, the open discussion of events in Hungary and Russia, even in *Unità* which, unlike *Humanité*, is often worth reading – all this greatly impressed Sartre. Here he met as a reality the possibility of a revolutionary party, less dogmatic in matters of the mind and less anti-intellectual than the French.

Sartre's sympathy for 'the more liberal' communist parties and trends in Poland and Italy, however, conflicts curiously with his 'ultra-bolshevism', expressed in unreserved sympathy for China as the home of genuine revolution untainted by bourgeois elements.[12] Is it possible to encourage at one and the same time everything in communism that does away with its insulation from the society around it, as well as everything that can make it into an elemental revolutionary force? In his major works Sartre justified the totalitarian element in communism, even if in philosophy he made reservations about what he calls his existentialist ideology, to

suffers from the brusque manner characteristic of French communists. A more comprehending attitude might perhaps have made it easier for him to evolve as he must have wished. Perhaps one is also entitled to blame him for failing to recognise that the demanding severity of the French party vis-à-vis the intellectuals is the expression of real respect for them.' (Jean Rony: 'Sartre et la politique', *Nouvelle Critique*, March 1966). The phrases used to express this 'real respect' to Sartre were 'agent of the FBI' and 'police philosopher'. In the first of the *Entretiens sur la politique*, the document of the *Rassemblement Démocratique Révolutionnaire*, Sartre mentioned three approaches by the communists which all ended in increased public abuse; he saw this as some form of natural law regulating the relationship between the PCF and independent intellectuals. In *Qu'est-ce que la littérature?* he had written: 'The policy of Stalinist communism is irreconcilable with the honest exercise of the literary profession.'

[12] An Italian Marxist recognized this contradiction in Sartre's attitude towards 'liberal' communism: 'Sartre's attempt at an existentialist renewal of Marxism has merely produced an internal revision of the "idealist voluntarism" that was the ideological background of Stalinism. Starting from the assumption that pluralism alienates, Sartre ridicules those democratic techniques (elections, division of powers, etc.) to which destalinisation itself appealed' (Pietro Chiodi, *Sartre e il marxismo*, 1965, p. 16).

be kept until Marxism itself becomes more intellectually alive. Enthusiasm for the unsophisticated force of pre-industrial peoples and for the open, intellectually liberal communism of Italy, do not go well together. But if Sartre ever recognised this contradiction – I find no sign in his writings that he did so – his visit to Cuba might have convinced him of the possibility of reconciling the apparently irreconcilable.

Castro's Cuba! Anyone who wishes to prove from the striking contradictions in Sartre's thought that ideas like his cannot be used as the foundation for a state may have logic on his side but finds himself in the position of the visitor to the zoo who, in front of the giraffe's cage, exclaims 'There is no such animal.' Because Cuba's reality corresponds to Sartre's Utopia. Sartre's long report on Cuba in *France-Soir* – it has appeared as a book in Spanish but not in French – combines dogmatic statements, questionable statistics, and psychological insights. In Castro, the son of landowners who becomes the leader of rebellious anti-bourgeois masses, he saw the personification of his Götz from *Le Diable et le bon Dieu*, and one who was moreover less bloodthirsty than the man of the peasant wars as he had portrayed him. In Castro's revolution he grasped the importance of the sense of resentment which played a greater part in Cuba's relations with the Americans than economic exploitation. Havana, he said, had become a brothel for American holidaymakers and many Cubans were ashamed of this. Castro brought about the revolution of racial equality; he himself remained spontaneity incarnate, comparable to the volatile character of Sartre's own political writings. What Sartre saw here was a very radical revolution which did not prohibit avant-garde developments in art and literature but, like the Russian revolution in its early days, allowed them to flourish. Unpredictability, encouragement of avant-garde elements, an urge to experiment at the expense of the economy, an ability to admit his own mistakes, references to Marxism-Leninism without submitting to the apparatus of the Old Guard of party functionaries, perpetual militancy – these are aspects of Fidel Castro's activity which were bound to appeal to Sartre.

So many happenings in the West and the East took a course completely contrary to Sartre's expectations – suffice it to recall his hopes for genuine revolutionary socialism in Algeria – that it is only fair to remember that in Cuba (at first) everything came true. Fidel Castro is Jean-Paul Sartre in power. Perhaps that is why Castroism is not a very happy and, in that form, not a very permanent state of affairs; but that is another story. Sartre established a different relationship with Cuba from that with the Soviet Union, and his report, in spite of its one-sidedness,[13] is on a very different level from that of the articles which he wrote on his travels in the Soviet Union.

What Sartre wrote about Russia in *Libération* dogmatically and with violent attacks on those journalists who saw things differently, must, with all respect for the great philosopher, be described as silly. In 1954 he found complete freedom of criticism; he said the Russians were so modern and objective in their approach that they never criticised persons but only measures; that whereas elsewhere people complained about 'the' government, the Russians complained about 'our' government. He noted joyfully that writers who had been expelled from their union still had the opportunity of 're-habilitating themselves by writing better books'.

Sartre as a traveller with political leanings and inclinations can appear ridiculous; but it is also important to notice that in such reports, as in many of his polemics, the quality of his output suffers severely, and it must be said in this context that not only are his reports inaccurate and vague, but that in his personal polemics, with his aggressive verve, he can be

[13] There were also some curious remarks, as for example the one about Castro's army: 'This army is dissolving itself and setting itself up. It sets itself up by dissolving itself. It dissolves itself by installing itself.' And about the *barbudos*: 'Most regular armies order their men to shave and it is no coincidence that these armies are incapable of winning a popular war. In the Sierra the beards conquered the clean-shaven, and the art of war was ridiculed.' Cited in Ludwig Marcuse, *Aus den Papieren eines bejahrten Philosophiestudenten.*

unfair and vicious, readily dismissing both individuals and whole groups as curs, as sub-human. Those who know Sartre personally say that he is generous, approachable, unaffected, a patient listener. But the reader knows that he enjoys the spectacle of unrestrained political violence and that in this sphere he knows no inhibitions. In a review of the third volume of Simone de Beauvoir's memoirs, Maria Craipeau objected to the author's approval of the internment in a labour camp of Pasternak's friend Ivinskaya and her daughter. Sartre's letter in *France Observateur* (December 12, 1963) contained the following passage:

> What right have you to question what Simone de Beauvoir says about Pasternak's friend? Have you been to the Soviet Union? Have you conducted an enquiry as we have? As regards the Soviets, naïvety today takes the form of automatic mistrust. It is the reflex of Pavlov's dog which salivates when it hears the sound of a flute. You foam at the mouth at the sound of the words 'Soviet Russia'. . . . You will die empty-handed.[14]

The conclusion that everything that the bourgeoisie criticises in the Soviet Union must for that very reason be the propaganda of *salauds* explains the failure of *Nekrassov*, a weak political play intended as a satire on the anti-communist newspaper world of Paris. The point of the play is the dissemination by this press of news of the fall of a police chief because one evening he fails to attend the opera. After Beria's fall this denunciation of the way in which capitalist legends are made no longer seemed quite so comic.[15]

[14] Typical also of Sartre's polemical style is his reply to Pierre Naville (a respected Marxist and contributor to *Les Temps modernes*): 'Naville's article is nothing. It is a poisonous nothing. . . . With the aid of one falsification, two contradictions, and a lie he has succeeded in concocting this inflated article whose only aim is to abuse. . . . I have always been of the opinion that even in the most vigorous debates we should preserve a tone of politeness and comradeship.' *Les Temps modernes*, March/April 1956, reprinted in *Situations VII*, pp. 129, 135, 136.

[15] 'In this play about the Paris press there is no communist newspaper – for which such a crude trick on the part of the reactionaries would have been a godsend – and there are no communists, just as Sartre is no com-

There has been only one phase in Sartre's political activity during which, together with his intellectual friends among whom he then still numbered David Rousset, he founded a movement of his own, the *Rassemblement démocratique révolutionnaire*, which he hoped would become an independent political factor.[16] The failure of this movement is described in Simone de Beauvoir's novel *Les Mandarins* which, although it contains distortions and even anachronisms, accurately catches the atmosphere. A decisive factor in Sartre's development was the realisation that it is impossible to entice the masses away from the communists, however aloof and clumsy they might be. It was impossible to establish a political revolutionary force, alongside and independent of the Communist Party; hence it was necessary partly to support and partly to influence that party. Even after November 1956 Sartre did not resign from the communist-controlled writers' association CEN, when the non-communists were leaving it in large numbers.

The communists are trying – recently with growing fervour – to reconcile themselves to Sartre as he is. Dialogues with Christians, dialogues with existentialists – this is the new

munist. Communism is an *idée fixe* of the anti-communists and a hope of the proletariat, in any case something beyond history and reality with which no dispute is possible.' Herbert Lüthy: 'Jean-Paul Sartre am Trapez', 1955; now in *Nach dem Untergang des Abenlandes.*

[16] The document of this period is *Entretiens sur la politique* between Jean-Paul Sartre, David Rousset, and Gérard Rosenthal. In it Sartre quotes Elie Halévy's *History of Socialism in the Nineteenth Century*: 'Socialism has from the start suffered from a contradiction. On the one hand it claims to be the heir of the ideology of 1789, and on the other it aims at a state-controlled authoritarian economy and thus at a totalitarian organization of society.' He comments: 'There is nobody today who is not conscious of this contradiction and does not seek to eliminate it by a new synthesis. This is the aim of the RDR, and this is what we call *concrete freedom.* . . . Concrete thought is the thought of a group of producers or consumers who take as their starting point the necessities of production within the enterprise concerned, and of consumption within the framework of needs and purchasing power. SUCH IDEAS CANNOT BE WRONG. There may well be mistakes of detail but not of principle; because what these producers, these consumers, are doing is to express what they *are.*'

slogan and it is very difficult to determine whether this in fact represents a move towards greater intellectual tolerance or merely a tactical manœuvre. This reservation also holds good for Aragon's protest against the sentences on Siniavsky and Daniel. What one can say is that all such gestures on the part of communist intellectuals find a resounding echo in France. Sartre has sharply attacked individual communists – for example his former pupil Kanapa, whom in *Les Temps modernes* he called a cretin,[17] with the result that Kanapa himself was compelled to apologise for his form of polemics. In March 1966 the communist organ *La Nouvelle critique* devoted almost an entire issue to Sartre, observing (no doubt primarily for internal consumption) that Sartre, whatever one might think of him, was a 'world famous personality', and that people abroad could not understand why the French communists attacked him. The harmful effect of this 'now outdated spirit of dogmatism' in past disputes is also admitted. Much of the communist criticism of Sartre bears a striking resemblance to the criticism made of him in the bourgeois or non-revolutionary camp. Sartre is interested in the activist group and shows little concern for the form of state. It is never clear what the difference between a democratic and a totalitarian system means to him, and whether the state in its continuity does not belong to the world of the serial product, of the 'practico-inert'. His confused attitude towards the structure of a regime therefore irritates bourgeois and bolshevik alike.

In an article entitled 'Literature Breathes', Julien Gracq has shown that Sartre's existentialist 'No' must make him as

---

[17] Kanapa had attacked both *Les Temps modernes* and *Preuves*, the journal sponsored by the Congress for Cultural Freedom, as though they formed a common front. Sartre's anger was primarily directed against this shameful 'amalgam'. But in the third volume of her memoirs Simone de Beauvoir names *Preuves* (which supported Algerian independence and whose offices were damaged by a plastic bomb attack by the OAS), together with two journals of the extreme Right which sympathized with the OAS. This way round the 'amalgam' was permitted.

intolerable to the communists as to the bourgeoisie. Gracq defined this 'No' as one which is

> undoubtedly marked more by strong emotions than by systematic thought, a No which comes partly from the bowels, as Sartre made explicit with the title of his first book, *La Nausée*. Within the span of a few years he has been the cause of the biggest discharge of resentment known in our literature for a long time, and this resentment is radical. A No to the physical world, to nature – which is obscene, which grows like a cancer, 'a senseless too-much', and disgusting to the point of nausea: this is the main theme of *La Nausée*. A No to others, to conscience, to one's nearest – this is the hell of *Huis clos*. A No to society as it is: this is the meaning of the whole of his journalistic activity – and a No, I am convinced, to any possible form of society ... a No to procreation, to sexuality, as being sticky, insidious, and disgusting. A No even to literary fame, the last refuge of the writer in revolt: and a No to the misunderstanding which results in a book surviving its author.

From this point of view it is possible to understand Sartre's 'No' to the Nobel literature prize which the Italian communist Quasimodo had accepted before him and which Sholokhov accepted after him. The urge to reject a 'bourgeois' honour was stronger than the desire to make a resounding revolutionary speech in Stockholm or to hand the prize money to some group with which he sympathised, such as the 'Castroist' maquis in Venezuela. Sartre's decision to refuse the prize is of course not open to criticism – Gracq himself had refused the Prix Goncourt for reasons of principle – but it belongs to an individualist tradition of protest and has nothing whatever in common with the behaviour of a communist intellectual.

In French politics Sartre has in recent years become increasingly erratic. After the establishment of Algerian independence and the defeat of the OAS (which had badly damaged his own house by a plastic bomb attack), no major issue remained, and the attempt to distinguish between the radical anti-western foreign policy he wanted to see and the 'pseudo-radical' foreign policy pursued by the Gaullists involves fine shades of difference rather than genuine indignation.[18]

Most of all, however, Sartre is disappointed by the fact that the French proletariat is becoming gradually less proletarian. The masses have no wish to overthrow the bourgeoisie which he, as he has written, 'will hate until his last breath'; they want to belong to it. The welfare state and Americanisation under a patriarchial regime give the masses something, but they give nothing to Sartre and intellectuals of his kind. Sartre's abhorrence of a stultifying and corrupting mass civilisation which has taken the goodness out of the revolution is in many ways appealing. It can, however, be supported by aristocratic as easily as by revolutionary arguments. This distaste is no mere caprice; only it cannot be combined with political demands in the name of the masses and with militant aims. Hence the increasing inconsistency of his comments. *Les Temps modernes* vigorously rejected Mitterrand as presidential candidate; yet soon afterwards Sartre recommended him.[19] The Federation of the Left and the communists are accused of political incompetence, but no analysis, such as might be expected from a monthly journal, is even attempted of this Left and the reasons for its impotence. Since the series *Les Communistes et la paix*, the gap between the historical militancy of revolutionary-minded

[18] In its anxiety to have nothing to do with de Gaulle's foreign policy, the leading article in *Les Temps modernes* of March 1963, presumably written by Sartre, uses terms which are worth reproducing in French: '*Finalement on aime bien ce "personnage" qui rend enfin à la France "sa place dans le monde" même et peut-être surtout si cette place est celle d'une emmerdeuse . . . Tel est pourtant le piège gaulliste: faire croire qu'un comportement erratique possède un sens positif et secret.*'

[19] 'This man [Mitterrand] is the candidate of the Left only to the extent that he personifies its decay . . . To support him would be folly or treachery' (leading article in *Les Temps modernes*, November 1965); 'To vote for Mitterrand does not mean voting *for* him but *against* the rule of one individual and *against* the retreat of the socialists to the Right' (Sartre in *Le Monde* December 4, 1965).

intellectuals and the 'passivity of masses' who refuse to be mobilised politically for incomprehensible aims has become more and more obvious.[20]

What has always been important for Sartre is not the content of politics alone but its style; not what happens but how and through whom. When de Gaulle put an end to the Algerian war Sartre received the news with indifference. It was no longer a victory of the French people against its colonialist bourgeoisie. Simone de Beauvoir speaks in her memoirs of the sadness and disappointment, of the morning-after-the-night-before feeling which contrasted strangely with the Algerian mood of victory.

What will happen to Sartre's politics in the French 'welfare state', in which the class struggles take place between state employees and state enterprises, while there is usually peace in the private sector? The Fifth Republic has done away with colonialism except for a few relics, and the Left opposes Gaullist foreign policy only on the question whether France should be an atomic power. This foreign policy could be endangered by a victory of the Left, an unlikely eventuality. *Les Temps modernes* writes with profound contempt about 'Brandt-Wilson-Nenni', describing them all as lackeys. Hence for them there is no real alternative to the Gaullists.

Today more than ever Sartre's politics are pure protest politics, preserving principles and hope in the logic of history as understood by Marxism, and renouncing any expectation of political victory in the foreseeable future. Now, when faith in the prospects of any form of active militancy is vanishing, the moment has perhaps come for more profound political and historical analysis. This at any rate was what Marx and Engels did when the tide of revolution ebbed. But Sartre has turned to his great work on Flaubert and has come back to his very own theme, that of the bourgeois who hates the

---

[20] 'Nowhere is the opposition between Right and Left as charged with prestige as in France, but nowhere is it more ambiguous; French conservatism expresses itself even in ideology.' Raymond Aron, *L'Opium des Intellectuels*, 1955, p. 42.

bourgeoisie but cannot find roots in any other class. This is how he has already presented Baudelaire. But in the nineteenth century there were big mass movements and France's social history was then the most violent in the world. If an entire people becomes bourgeois, does not the individual intellectual's hatred of the bourgeoisie, expressed in aesthetic and intellectual terms, become topical again? Sartre's fascination with Flaubert prompts this question.

Sartre's influence and political impact on young French intellectuals is no longer what it was. Among sociologists and 'structuralists' new *maîtres à penser* have emerged, and the synthesis between Marxism and structuralism, as attempted by Louis Althusser for example, is of more interest today than Sartre's Existential-Marxism. In an interview published in *L'Arc*,[21] Sartre took issue with these new tendencies and accused their representatives of misunderstanding temporality, that is, history itself. Structure for him means the area of the 'pratico-inert', of rigidity. But in this Sartre no longer finds the same echo as of old. The situation is different as regards the communists. Co-existence with Sartre has become a major task for them – more than for the 'bourgeois'. *La Nouvelle critique* asks him to remember that today an individual can no longer, as in Voltaire's day, be a great thinker; the 'collective brain of the party' alone plays such a role. But the very fact that this communist journal should have to defend itself so strongly against the 'Voltairean fame' of one man shows the awkwardness of the situation. Today 'world communism' is no longer the monolith which Sartre justified and to which he even granted the right of military attack. It is in a state of political and intellectual disintegration. Both Sartre's philosophy and his political ideas are today part of the ferment of the changing communist world. In spite of Sartre's justification of political dogmatism, his effect in the communist world, including both groups in power and groups in opposition, lies in the sphere of philosophy and criticism. The book of the Polish Marxist,

[21] Special number on Sartre, November 1966.

Adam Schaff, on Sartre and Marxism is one witness among many of the intellectually stimulating impact of Sartre's ideas.[22] The various degrees of independence from basically accepted communist doctrine are not a major issue in the West today. No one there feels roused to indignation or belligerency by this sworn enemy of liberalism and the middle classes. Sartre's influence, and this more through his whole work and his indirect intellectual effect than through his political utterances proper, is greater in the communist world. In the East his distinction between rigid and open Marxism is topical. The effect of his whole work is more to contribute to discussion in the communist world than to revolution in the bourgeois world. This is not what he intended. But a man like Sartre, who wants to think historically, ought not to be unhappy about this historical paradox.

The French upheavals of May 1968, a student revolt acting as a detonator to a general strike; the occupation of Czecho-slovakia by a Russian-led holy alliance against 'socialism with a human face'; the continued state of war between Israel and Arab countries; and equally a growing need to reflect on his own previous attitudes and options – all this has prompted the thoughts expressed by Sartre in more recent interviews and essays, five of which merit particular notice.

1. In a long interview with *Le Nouvel Observateur* – published on March 3, 1969, – Sartre warned French students not to accept any plan of reforms such as the one conceived by Edgar Faure, then French Minister of Education, and unanimously adopted by the National Assembly.

[22] 'In 1951 when we were making plans for a Marxist offensive against non-Marxist trends in our philosophy, existentialism was completely ignored. . . . Only a few years later – 1956 and 1957 – it had become a real force, particularly in Marxist circles. . . . Compared with Marxism, existentialism not only sees philosophic problems in other terms, using a different terminology, reflecting a different *Weltanschauung*, but also reflects a completely different world of thought and feeling.' Adam Schaff, *Marx oder Sartre? Versuch einer Philosophie des Menschen* (Frankfurt, 1966).

'There is need to fight violence with violence, [said Sartre], we have in common with you the revolutionary negation, the rejection of any kind of participation. Parents, learn that your sons have become revolutionaries because your cowardice has determined their fate. They have nothing to say any more to those defeated and decaying children who call themselves adults. We who say this are also adults, but either less corrupted or more conscious of our corruption.'

In the same interview Sartre repudiated any kind of 'pure' culture divorced from immediate practical action. 'True, to change the world it is necessary to understand it, but anything which does not lead directly to praxis is constriction (*contrainte*).'

Here, the author of *Critique of dialectical reason* follows closely his previously expressed thought, his fear that institutions will immediately harden and expropriate any revolution of its virtues. In May 1968 Sartre interviewed Cohn-Bendit in a spirit of humility, convinced that he had little to teach and much to learn. Even so, Sartre's extreme commitment to the 'spirit of May' did not bring his books into favour with the French students, who turned rather to the writings of Herbert Marcuse and of Henri Lefèbvre.

2. *Quaderni del Medio Oriente* (Milan) published a conversation between Sartre and its editor, Arturo Schwarz, which was re-printed in the French Jewish magazine *L'Arche* of October 1969. On the conflict in the Near East, Sartre maintains his objectivity and does not follow the French New Left which with very few exceptions has adopted the Arab cause and transferred hero worship from Guevara and Regis Debray to El Fatah. Sartre says it is absurd to pretend that 'Israel is an imperialist state and the Arabs are socialists including their feudal states'. However, he reproaches Israel with becoming 'more capitalist and wedded more to the market economy' and accuses the Israeli press of supporting the dictatorship of the Greek colonels (does it really?). Sartre thinks, however, that the destruction of minorities (i.e. the Jewish State inside the Arab world) does not lead to any

progress, 'any more than Stalinism can lead to socialism'. 'In any case Israel has not been the aggressor' and Sartre speaks of 'objective complicity between Americans and Russians just as in the case of Biafra there was objective complicity between the Russians and the British'.

3. In the *New Left Review* (November-December, 1969), Sartre retraces in a long interview the 'itinerary of his thought'. This interview was later published in *Le Nouvel Observateur* of January 16, 1970, under the title 'Sartre against Sartre'. The English version is more complete and interesting than the French one which had probably to be shortened for considerations of space. Here is one of the passages missing in *Le Nouvel Observateur*: 'When I discovered the class struggle, this was a *true* discovery, in which I now believe totally, in the very form of the descriptions which Marx gave of it. Only the epoch has changed: otherwise it is the same struggle with the same classes and the same road to victory.' On anarchic individualism Sartre thinks – this passage too is not to be found in *Le Nouvel Observateur* – that it can lead to some kind of madness and be a danger, if not to the individual concerned, then to society.

On the Chinese cultural revolution Sartre admits that he is not well informed but observes: 'To proclaim total freedom of individuals inside a group and to put at the same time into the heads of these individuals those pebbles called "Mao's thoughts" is utterly contradictory.' As to the French Communist Party, Sartre calls it 'the largest conservative party in France', and he goes on to say that one ought to stay revolutionary and patient 'with the same persistence as the Vietnamese'. Sartre insists on the danger of a 'bureaucratic deterioration' of a revolution which would come about in any Western country, and he announces his intention to write some kind of a 'political testament'. By this he does not mean a piece of advice but the kind of testament which belongs to the end of a life. He wants to show how a man may come into politics and be changed by it, 'what errors I have committed and what has resulted from them'.

4. Sartre's introduction to a book by the Czech writer

Antonin Liehm (*Trois générations*) – a series of talks with Czech and Slovak intellectuals before the Soviet occupation – is called 'The socialism which came in from the cold', and is one of Sartre's most brilliant and incisive essays. He refers to the Soviet political economic system as to '*la chose*', the thing, just as before he referred to China's 'numeralised order'. He even questions the merits of the Yugoslav reforms on '*autogestion*': 'It becomes meaningless as long as there is a centralised political organisation in the hands of a privileged group.' The trials and confessions, the institutionalised lie, the atomisation of individuals, all such things to his mind are not degenerations of a system but its true and inevitable logic, its own perfection. The Russians, Sartre now thinks, 'could not act otherwise' than they did in August 1968. He calls on the Left to shed all illusions of moralism and re-formism. The machine cannot be mended. People have to take possession of the 'thing' and throw it into the sewer (*au rebut*). From now on, Sartre says, we have to think how to get rid of old structures and create new ones while preventing the future from looking like *their* 'kind of socialism'.

5. *Les Temps modernes* of January 1970, publishes a conversation between Sartre and unnamed members of the Italian group 'Manifesto' – an opposition inside the Italian P.C. from which many members have been expelled. Here Sartre returns to consider his position of 1952 when he felt that the main enemy was American imperialism and that one had to take sides with its enemy the Soviet Union. Now since 1956 it has become clear, he says, that Russia is also imperialist, and this, he adds, does not 'constitute a value judgment' but a statement of fact. Sartre feels he has therefore to consider 'the contradiction with my own positions of 1952'. Tantalisingly he adds: 'I have already started to write an analysis of the Soviet Union under Stalin. It belongs to the second volume of my *Critique of dialectical reason* but this volume will probably never be published.'

At one point, Sartre talks just as he did twenty years ago in saying that 'French capitalism' has kept alive thousands of small enterprises which are not technically rational but which maintain a large sector of conservativism. This personification of capitalism as a decision-making entity becomes even more obscure when Sartre adds: 'Tendencies to integration do not annul the profound diversifications of structural situations.' He comes close to Marcuse in suggesting that the problem in advanced capitalist states is not so much real need – or what in his *Critique* he called '*la rareté*' (scarcity) – but rather alienation caused by creation of artificial consumer needs. The only instance of this he quotes, however, is the automobile. His own utopia, he admits, is the withering away not only of the state but of politics altogether through a full exercise of self-government at every level. This, he says, should at least be a working hypothesis. As for the contradiction between a hardened institution such as a communist party and the need for openness, imagination and flux, Sartre sees, for the time being, no way of resolving it.

What can one conclude from these recent statements? Sartre is no longer in favour of any kind of left revolution overthrowing capitalist states but is deeply antagonistic to all totalitarian regimes. He calls for revolution in the East as well as in the West. In the West, Sartre considers the deeper frustrations and alienations rather than the direct economic problem. Although he believes that the class struggle has remained the same, he does not mind having to 'deprive Billancourt of its hopes' if these hopes can lead to Stalinism. He considers his own earlier statements on the identity of working class, communist party and Soviet Union as outdated and irrelevant. Sartre denounces the self-perpetuating bourgeois culture and against it favours the most radical youth revolt and 'cultural revolution'.

However, in relation to communism, his objections are partly of a liberal, partly of a libertarian, type. Although he does not advise the young to study history, except so far as it is linked to immediate 'praxis', he himself reconsiders the history which he has lived through. He is more aware than ever of his own contradictions and, despite his sometimes fanatical calls for extreme action, he increasingly appears as a troubled conscience in troubled times. From revolution at all costs against bourgeois society he has moved to 'revolution but not at the cost of being afterwards burdened by a totalitarian system'. Sartre is torn between revolutionary activist commitment and critical meditation. For many years a committed thinker, he now seems, rather more than in the past, committed to thought itself. And yet, his latest dramatic commitment to a Maoist newspaper in France, on the occasion of the imprisonment of its editors, prompts one to wonder whether his deepest attachments are not to a cause which can command his mind and heart beyond the exercise of political scepticism and intellectual self-doubt.

HERBERT MARCUSE

Maurice Cranston

HERBERT MARCUSE

Maurice Cranston

I

In the year 1955 Professor Herbert Marcuse published a book
of radiant optimism. It bore the modest title *Eros and Civilisation: a Philosophical Enquiry into Freud*,[1] but what it contained was a spirited rejoinder to Freud's belief that civilisation
depends on repression. Marcuse argued that a non-repressive
civilisation is a possibility. We had only to remove the repressive elements which belong to political domination, he
suggested, and men could live peaceably together in freedom.
Moreover, once the unnecessary repressive forces were
eliminated, human instincts would be transformed and lose
their destructive features. Indeed, Marcuse not only used the
word 'would', he sometimes used the word 'will', notably
towards the end of his book. For instance, having predicted
that the Freudian death-wish would vanish in a non-
repressive culture, Marcuse wrote:

> 'Death would cease to be an instinctive goal. It remains
> a fact, perhaps, even an ultimate necessity – but a necessity
> against which the unrepressed energy of mankind *will*
> protest, against which it *will* wage its greatest struggle'
> [my italics]. (p. 215.)

The optimism of this treatise is not marginal, for the central purpose of its argument was to reverse Freud's pessimism.
What Marcuse set out to do was to refute the implication of
Freudian theory 'that the humanitarian ideals of socialism
are humanly unattainable'. He resisted the use of the word
'utopian' as a word of condemnation, whether by psychoanalysts or anyone else:

[1] *Eros and Civilisation: a Philosophical Enquiry into Freud* (Beacon Press
and Vintage Books, 1955).

'Theology and philosophy today compete with each other in celebrating death as an existential category; perverting a biological fact into an ontological essence, they bestow transcendental blessing on the guilt of mankind which they help to perpetuate – they betray the promise of utopia.' (p. 216.)

Marcuse himself in *Eros and Civilisation* upheld the promise of utopia. Only he did not sustain his buoyant optimism. In his next book, *One-Dimensional Man,*[2] his mood was lugubrious and his conclusion despairing. This book is a study of, or more exactly an attack upon, modern and especially American industrial civilisation. On the last page Marcuse wrote:

'The critical theory of society possesses no concepts which could bridge the gap between the present and its future; holding no promise and showing no success, it remains loyal to those who, without hope, have given and give their life to the Great Refusal. . . . *Nur um der Hoffnungslosen willen ist uns die Hoffnung gegeben* [Only for the sake of the hopeless is hope given to us]. . . .' (p. 257.)

In an essay written at about this same time for a book on Babeuf,[3] Marcuse employed the word 'utopian' in its pejorative sense. He did not dispute Babeuf's belief that the political sentiments held by a 'misled, indoctrinated and ignorant populace are not to be regarded as the people's real will, and that the establishment of a "real Republic" involved acting (and writing) against the majority.' Indeed, as I shall presently show, this is very much Marcuse's own opinion. Even so, Marcuse wrote at the end of this short essay: 'A theory and strategy which was quite unrealistic but not utopian in 1796 appears as utterly utopian today.'

Utterly utopian. And yet not too utterly utopian to prevent Marcuse's taking it up, and promoting it in his subsequent writings. The curious thing is that in the past few years Marcuse's old optimism has returned to him. Fortified, per-

---

[2] *One-Dimensional Man* (Beacon Press, 1964).

[3] *In Defense of Gracchus Babeuf.* Edited by J. A. Scott, with an essay by Herbert Marcuse (University of Massachusetts Press, 1967).

haps, by the acclaim of rebellious students throughout the world, if not by the interest of the press, which he despises, Marcuse has recovered the spirit which animated *Eros and Civilisation*. But with optimism and utopian aspiration, there has also appeared in Marcuse's writings a new vein of impatience, intolerance, and the will to violence, such as often seems to go together with the more hopeful kind of left-wing yearning.[4] Evidence of Marcuse's later state of mind we find in *A Critique of Pure Tolerance*,[5] published in 1966 in a peculiar format, bound in black like a prayer book or missal and perhaps designed to compete with *The Thoughts of Chairman Mao* as devotional reading at student sit-ins. This is Marcuse's most popular work so far, and his most disturbing.

The argument is simple. The ideal of tolerance belongs to the liberal, democratic tradition which has exhausted itself. What Marcuse likes to call liberalist society is based, he says, on a form of domination so subtle that the majority accept and even will their servitude. In such a condition tolerance as traditionally understood serves the cause of domination. Therefore, Marcuse concludes, a new kind of toleration is needed – tolerance of the Left, tolerance of subversion, tolerance of revolutionary violence, but intolerance of the Right, intolerance of existing institutions, intolerance of any opposition to socialism. His words are beautifully candid:

'As to the scope of this tolerance and intolerance, it would extend to the stage of action as well as of discussion and propaganda, of deed as well as of word. . . . The whole post-fascist period is one of clear and present danger. Consequently, true pacification requires the withdrawal of tolerance before the deed, at the stage of communication in word, print and picture. Such extreme suspension of the right of free speech and free assembly is indeed justified only if the whole of society is in extreme danger. I maintain

[4] See Karl Popper's essay, 'Utopia and Violence', in *Conjectures and Refutations* (Routledge, 1962).

[5] *A Critique of Pure Tolerance*. Essays by Robert Paul Wolff, Barrington Moore, Jr, and Herbert Marcuse (Beacon Press, 1966).

that our society is in such an emergency situation, and that it has become the normal state of affairs.' (p. 109.)

Marcuse is eager to see this policy of intolerance adopted without delay:

'Withdrawal of tolerance from regressive movements *before* they can become active; intolerance even toward thought, opinion and word, and finally, intolerance in the opposite direction, that is, toward the self-styled conservatives, to the political Right – these anti-democratic notions respond to the actual development of the democratic society which has destroyed the basis for universal tolerance. The conditions under which tolerance can still become a liberating and humanising force have still to be created.' (p. 110.)

II

I want to examine the stages by which Herbert Marcuse reached the point of uttering these aggressively illiberal propositions. From one perspective they are not what might have been expected of him. For Marcuse is a scholar, a thinker, and a German Jew, a blood brother of the millions who fell victims to political intolerance in the gas chambers. Enough, one might have supposed, to breed some appreciation of that 'liberalist' society which resisted Nazism, and by giving Marcuse asylum, saved him from the same fate. But no. Marcuse has a singularly lofty attitude to the gas chambers: 'The world of the concentration camps was not an exceptionally monstrous society. . . . What we saw there was the image, and in a sense the quintessence, of the infernal society into which we are plunged every day.'

There may be readers who would find nothing in Marcuse surprising. For Marcuse is, or claims to be, an Hegelian; and in the historical accounts of Hobhouse, Popper, Camus and Talmon, Hegel is the central figure in the tradition of German totalitarian fanaticism, so that the Hegelian Marcuse simply takes his place with Fichte, Marx, Bismarck, Hitler, in that sinister succession. I do not myself believe that Hegel can properly be seen as a forerunner of Hitler. He was a constitutional monarchist, with a firm belief in reason and law. But there is undoubtedly a vulgarised 'Hegelian' tradition which contributed something to the success of both Nazism and Fascism, though little compared to the wholly anti-rational, anti-philosophical passions of the *popolo* and the *Volk*. Marcuse himself published in 1941 a book, *Reason and Revolution*,[6] intended to defend Hegel against the charge of being an originator of 'fascist ideas'; but what price that defence now, when Marcuse himself proclaims opinions more extreme than any that have been ascribed to Hegel by Hegel's most uncharitable critics?

But let us return to the evolution of Marcuse's theories. Of his biography I know little but what is to be found in books of reference: that he was born in Germany in 1898, studied philosophy at Berlin and Freiburg, was active in the revolutionary movement f Rosa Luxemburg, helped to found (with Max Horkheimer and T. W. Adorno) the 'Frankfurt School' of Marxist sociology, left Germany in 1933 to work at the Institut of Social Research in Geneva, then emigrated to America where he has been either a research fellow or a professor at Columbia, Harvard, Brandeis and California universities. In this article I am concerned only with the ideas set forth in his published works. The earliest one to which he himself appears to attach importance, naming it in the bibliography of *Reason and Revolution*, is one entitled '*Der Kampf gegen dem Liberalismus in der totalitären Staatsauffassung*' which was published in Paris in 1935 in the *Zeitschrift für Sozialforschung*,[7] a journal connected with the 'Frankfurt School' of sociology.

This is an essay which throws an important light on Marcuse's subsequent thinking. In the course of it he notes that exponents of Nazi, fascist and related 'heroic-*völkisch*'

---

[6] *Reason and Revolution* (New York, 1941; 2nd edn., Beacon Press, 1960, and Routledge, 1968).

[7] This essay, with other early writings of Marcuse, has been reproduced in translation in *Negations* (Beacon Press and Allen Lane, The Penguin Press, 1968).

irrationalist political ideologies all write bitterly against liberalism. But Marcuse suggests that these attacks are deceptive. For liberalism, he alleges, is deeply connected with fascism and the related creeds. Not only is liberalism 'at one with fascism in its fight against Marxian socialism', which is the common enemy of both liberalism and fascism, but the relationship is in truth more intimate. Liberalism, Marcuse writes, has to be understood as the ideology of capitalism in its competitive phase; when capitalism reaches the monopolistic stage, its ideology changes; and fascism is nothing other than liberalism transfigured to meet the need of an altered economic situation. Elsewhere, in his exposition of Hegel's political theory, Marcuse asserts that 'the gist of Hegel's analysis' of the development of the several stages of government is that 'liberal society necessarily gives birth to an authoritarian state'. (Hegel said nothing of the kind.) In this German essay, Marcuse advances as his own conclusion that 'it is liberalism that "produces" the total-authoritarian state out of itself, as its own consummation at a more advanced stage of development'; and he gives as 'evidence' in support of this conclusion what he does not blush to describe as 'a classic document illustrating the inner relationship between liberalist social theory and the (apparently so anti-liberal) totalitarian theory or state: a letter addressed to Mussolini by Gentile when the latter joined the Fascist Party, [saying] "a genuine liberal . . . must enrol in the legion of your followers"'.

This view of the relationship between liberalism and fascism, perverse as it is, and jejune, and at variance with all the testimony of history, Marcuse has never retracted, and his continued adherence to it does much to explain the peculiarity of his later theories.

Another significant clue to the working of Marcuse's mind may be found in the pages of *Reason and Revolution*, towards the end of the book, where he discusses the Victorian English Idealist philosopher, Bernard Bosanquet, and his *Philosophical Theory of the State* (1899):

'The principles of liberalism [Marcuse writes] are valid; the common interest cannot be other in the last analysis than the product of the multitude of freely developing individual selves in society. But the concrete forms of society that have developed since the nineteenth century have increasingly frustrated the freedom to which liberalism counsels allegiance. Under the laws that govern the social process, the free play of private initiative has wound up in competition among monopolies for the most part. . . . Bosanquet's *Philosophical Theory of the State* appeared when this transition from liberal to monopolistic capitalism had already begun. Social theory was faced with the alternative either of abandoning the principles of liberalism so that the existing social order might be maintained, or fighting the system in order to preserve the principles. The latter choice was implied in the Marxian theory of society.' (p. 397.)

This last sentence is crucial. Marcuse is saying that the principles of liberalism – freedom, individuality, progress – are good principles, but that liberalism which has always been willing to sacrifice them to defend property and the *status quo*, has now, in turning fascist, abandoned them entirely, while Marxian socialism has taken them over, and, unlike liberalism, is willing to do what is needed to uphold liberal principles in the twentieth century, namely, to overthrow existing society.

It is interesting to notice the date of the book in which Marcuse said all this. *Reason and Revolution* was written in 1940 and published in 1941, the years of the great Nazi-Soviet embrace, when *Humanité* tried to obtain a licence to publish in Paris under German auspices, the *GPU* was handing over Jews and other anti-Nazis to the Gestapo in Poland, and the only state effectively resisting Hitler and Mussolini was the homeland of liberal capitalism – and of Bernard Bosanquet – the British Empire. To have asserted *at that time* that Marxian socialism was the true custodian of liberal values, and to have repeated that Marxian socialism not liberalism was fascism's real enemy was surely to betray a remarkable unresponsiveness to the realities of the external world. However, such an unresponsiveness is, as we shall see, an enduring characteristic of Marcuse's mind and method.

III

It should be said at once that Marcuse's Marxism is not that of the Communist Party. In his book *Soviet Marxism*[8] he describes the prevailing Russian ideology as a genuine form of Marxism. 'The Stalinist reconstruction of Soviet society based itself on Leninism, which was a specific interpretation of Marxian theory and practice', Marcuse writes, but he criticises that 'reconstruction' because of its totalitarianism and repressiveness. There are times when he seems to regard the Soviet Union as simply another modern industrial society like the United States, objectionable for the same reasons. Now and again he suggests that the Soviet Union as a totalitarian system is even worse than America, or any democratic system, however defective:

> '...for the administered individual, pluralistic administration is far better than total administration. One institution might protect him against the other; one organisation might mitigate the impact of the other: possibilities of escape and redress can be calculated. The rule of law, no matter how restricted, is still infinitely safer than the rule above or without law.' (*One-Dimensional Man*, p. 51.)

Marcuse's hostility[9] to totalitarian socialism goes together, reasonably enough, with his belief that Marxism has taken

[8] *Soviet Marxism: a critical analysis* (Routledge, 1958).

[9] 'Hostility' is perhaps too strong a word. In a television interview (*Listener*, October 17, 1968), R. T. McKenzie asked Marcuse: 'Is it of concern to you, as a kind of neo-Marxist, that there doesn't seem to be any society based on Marxist-Leninist principles which so far has gotten near the idea of complete freedom of inquiry and debate?'

Marcuse replied: 'It may sound fantastic, but I do not take that as an invalidation of the idea of socialism. We can very well explain the reasons why this has been: under the conditions of so-called peaceful co-existence the construction of socialism is burdened with a huge defence budget which makes it practically impossible to take the direct route to socialism.'

over from liberalism the principles that liberalism has forsaken, notably freedom and individualism. Indeed Marcuse's 'Marxism' embodies principles even more advanced than these. His optimistic belief that a non-repressive civilisation is a possibility belongs less to liberalism than to anarchism. If a name had to be chosen for Marcuse's politics it would have to be 'Anarcho-Marxism'.

The reader who can relish irony as well as paradox may venture to consider what Marx himself might have thought of such a conjunction. For Marx met anarchism in the person of Michael Bakunin, his greatest rival for leadership of the Workers' International, and he hated it; he spoke of anarchism with the liveliest scorn. Bakunin believed in the possibility of a non-repressive civilisation, and he anticipated much that is to be found in the writings of Marcuse. Anarcho-Marxism is a fusion with Marxism of views that Marx himself regarded as wholly antithetical to his own. Marx in his tomb can have felt no qualms when the Spanish Communists in 1938 turned their guns on the Spanish Anarchists; if he was disturbed when the black-and-red flag was unfurled beside the red flag above the Sorbonne in 1968, he could doubtless forgive Daniel Cohn-Bendit and his friends for voicing the eternal desire of youth to have one's cake and eat it; but what Marx would say of Marcuse is something to baffle the imagination.

A certain discretion, or delicacy of feeling, prompts Marcuse to expound his anarchist views most fully, not in his writings on Marx, but in his book on Freud. His argument in *Eros and Civilisation* is a revision of Freud which Marcuse takes care to distinguish from the fashionable 'revisionist' or Neo-Freudian theories. Thus, whereas Erich Fromm, Karen Horney and the others seek to add a sociological dimension to the Freudian image of man, Marcuse claims to find the sociological and historical insight in Freud's own theory. He accuses the Neo-Freudians of distorting and emasculating Freud; of taking the sting out of Freud's own judgment on civilisation. The aim of their therapy, he says, is to make the patient adjust himself to the world as it is, and even though they may assign to society some of the blame for what is wrong, they treat the individual as the one who is really at fault. Marcuse adds: 'to the Neo-Freudian revisionist, the brute fact of societal repression has transformed itself into a "moral problem" – as it has done in conformist philosophy of all ages.'

I shall not go into the question of whether this attack is just. Erich Fromm, in particular, being himself a New Left personality, might well consider it unjust. I shall simply note that Marcuse addresses to the Neo-Freudian revisionists the same objection that ordinary Marxists use against Freud himself. Freud, they assert, fails to see neurosis as evidence of a sick society; but finding the defect in the individual, seeks to correct it by changing the individual while leaving society untouched. The ordinary Marxists reinforce this criticism by reference to Freud's known political views: Freud was as conservative as Thomas Hobbes, and for much the same reasons, namely that men were in such danger from the violence of human aggression that they would be wise to cling to whatever traditional defences they had. On this view, Freud's own psycho-analysis is, in Marcuse's phrase, 'a conformist philosophy'.

Marcuse offers a different reading of Freud; and by a method which he calls 'extrapolation', or an unfolding of the 'hidden implications' of Freud's theory, he attempts to develop a synthesis of psycho-analysis and socialism. It is Freud in his most cheerless moments that Marcuse fastens on to sustain his most optimistic conclusions. He protests that everyone takes for granted Freud's view that civilisation is based on the permanent subjugation of the human instincts, but that no one takes seriously enough Freud's question whether civilisation is worth what it has cost in suffering inflicted on individuals. Marcuse quotes Freud's words 'Happiness is not a cultural value'. Happiness lies in the free gratification of men's instinctual needs, which is incompatible with civilised society. The methodical sacrifice of libido, its rigidly enforced deflection to socially useful activities, *is* culture.

Because Freud speaks in these terms, Marcuse sees him as a profound and far-reaching critic of civilisation *as we know it*. At the same time Marcuse argues that Freud's theory provides reasons for rejecting Freud's own conclusion that culture as such necessarily depends on repression as he defines it. Briefly Marcuse's argument is as follows: Freud establishes that some degree of repression is necessary to any civilisation, but the extent of repression employed in the actual cultures known to history is far in excess of the amount that Freud shows to be necessary for civilisation as such to exist. In fact, Marcuse suggests, 'repressiveness is perhaps the more vigorously maintained the more unnecessary it becomes'. Marcuse then goes on to divide the concept of repression into what he calls *basic* repression and *surplus* repression. The *basic* repressions are the modifications of the human instincts that are necessary (and Marcuse agrees with Freud that some modifications at least are necessary) for the preservation of the human race in civilisation. *Surplus* repression comprises the restrictions needed for another purpose. And it is not difficult to guess what that purpose is. It is to maintain the social or class domination which characterises known societies. On the basis of this distinction, Marcuse puts forward both as realistic and as good Freudian sense his own belief that a non-repressive culture is possible – a non-repressive culture being understood as one from which surplus repression has been eliminated. And if anyone should suggest that civilisation would still be, in a very real sense, repressive so long as basic repression remained, Marcuse's answer is that once surplus repression is removed, human instincts themselves will begin to change, so that even basic repression will lose its importance.

The second modification that Marcuse introduces into Freudian psychology concerns the reality principle. Freud himself contrasted the reality principle with the pleasure principle and suggested that as the original animal instinctive man (seeking immediate satisfactions, joy and liberty) is transformed by culture into a self-controlled mature human (seeking security, accepting delayed satisfactions, restraint and work), so the reality principle takes the place of the pleasure principle as a man's governing value. Now Marcuse argues that this reality principle is not something biological or universal, but something to be understood in sociological and historical terms, for it is society, he says, which dictates the sacrifices and restraints that the individual must accept.

'The external world faced by the growing ego is at any stage a specific socio-historical organisation of reality, affecting the mental structure through specific societal agencies or agents', Marcuse writes, and he goes on to insist that however much Freud may justify the repressive organisation of the instincts on the grounds that the primary pleasure principle is irreconcilable with the reality principle, Freud at least 'expresses the historical fact that civilisation has progressed as organised *domination*'.

Marcuse continues: 'The "unhistorical" character of the Freudian concepts thus contains the element of its opposite: their historical substance must be recaptured, not by adding some sociological factors (as do the "cultural" Neo-Freudian schools) but by unfolding their own contents.' This task of unfolding – or extrapolation – Marcuse executes with the aid of a terminology unknown to Freud, but based on Freudian language. And just as he divides repression into 'basic' and 'surplus', so he now distinguishes the reality principle from what he calls the '*performance principle*'. His suggestion is that the reality principle takes different forms in different types of society (depending, as he puts it, on the 'mode of domination'); and he calls the form of reality principle which has governed the growth of our own civilisation, the 'performance principle' in order (as he explains) 'to emphasise that under its rule society is stratified according to the competitive economic performances of its members'.

Thus, with a brisk audacity, Marcuse uses this notion of a 'performance principle' to marry psycho-analysis to socialism:

'The performance principle, which is that of an acquisitive antagonistic society in the process of constant expansion, presupposes a long development during which domination has been increasingly rationalised; control over social labour now reproduces society on an enlarged scale and under improving conditions. For a long way, the interests of domination and the interests of the whole coincide; the profitable utilisation of the productive apparatus fulfils the needs and the faculties of the individual. For the vast majority of the population, the scope and mode of satisfaction are determined by their own labour; but their labour is work for an apparatus which they do not control, which operates as an independent power to which individuals must submit if they want to live. And it becomes the more alien the more specialised the division of labour becomes. Men do not live their own lives, but perform pre-established functions. While they work, they do not fulfil their own needs and faculties, but work in *alienation*.' (p. 41.)

This marriage or synthesis is not intended to yield any therapeutic technique. As the author explains, his aim is to contribute to the philosophy of psycho-analysis, not to psycho-analysis itself, and in his preface he suggests that the traditional frontiers between psychology and political or social theory have been 'made obsolete by the condition of man in the present era'. To put it rather more plainly, Marcuse's purpose is ideological. He holds that most of the repressions sustained in existing society are 'surplus', serving only the interests of political domination; further, that men can not only *afford* to throw off these surplus repressions, but their own condition is one of such hellish alienation that they *ought* to do so. What Marcuse holds out is a promise of liberty.

IV

Marcuse not only thinks this revolutionary development conceivable, he even indicates the manner of its realisation. Very much like Fourier, to whom he addresses a word of acknowledgment, Marcuse envisages the transformation of labour into pleasure as the solution to the problem of alienation. Again, like Fourier, Marcuse believes that this can be achieved only by a complete change in social institutions, a distribution of the social product according to need, the assignment of functions according to talent and the provision of 'attractive labour'. Marcuse praises Fourier for having noticed that the possibility of *le travail attrayant* 'derives above all from the release of libidinal forces', but he criticises Fourier for having proposed an authoritarian socialist community which retained the repressive element. Marcuse's objection to Fourier is Bakunin's objection, enlivened with a dressing of sex. Marcuse suggests that *le travail attrayant* is possible only if work is transformed into play; and work as free play 'cannot be subject to administration'. He continues:

> 'If pleasure is indeed in the act of working and not extraneous to it, such pleasure must be derived from the acting organs of the body and the body itself, activating the erotogenic zones or eroticising the body as a whole; in other words, it must be libidinal pleasure.' (p. 201.)

It is necessary at this point to remember that Marcuse sees as one essential feature of a non-repressive civilisation a change in the nature of sexuality itself. He thinks it important to demonstrate that the sexual instincts can, by virtue of their own dynamic, generate under changed social conditions lasting erotic relationships and even promote progress towards higher forms of civilised freedom. He is careful to explain that the social changes he has in mind involve not simply a release, but a transformation of the libido, a transformation 'from sexuality constrained under genital supremacy to erotisation of the entire personality'.

> 'It is a spread rather than an explosion of libido – a spread over private and societal relations which bridges the gap maintained between them by a repressive reality principle. This transformation of the libido would be the result of a societal transformation that released the free play of individual needs and faculties. By virtue of these

conditions the free development of transformed libido *beyond* the institutions of the performance principle differs essentially from the release of unconstrained sexuality *within* the dominion of these institutions. The latter process explodes *suppressed* sexuality; the libido continues to bear the mark of suppression and manifests itself in the hideous forms so well known in the history of civilisation; in the sadistic and masochistic orgies of desperate masses, of "society élites", of starved bands of mercenaries, of prison and concentration-camp guards. Such release of sexuality provides a periodically necessary outlet for unbearable frustration; it strengthens rather than weakens the roots of instinctual constraint; consequently, it has been used time and again as prop for suppressive régimes. In contrast the free development of transformed libido within transformed institutions, while eroticising previously tabooed zones, time, and relations, would *minimise* the manifestations of *mere* sexuality by integrating them into a far larger order, including the order of work. In this context, sexuality tends to its own sublimation: the libido would not simply reactivate pre-civilised and infantile stages but would also transform the perverted content of these stages.' (p. 184.)

Here, assuredly, is the voice of optimism; and it is an optimism based entirely on faith, for Marcuse offers no evidence whatsoever to justify his conclusions. The optimists of the eighteenth century at least gave some empirical grounds for their belief that a removal of religious taboos would produce better sexual relationships. They quoted the discovery by Bougainville and other voyagers of primitive societies where sexual freedom and happiness went together. But Marcuse offers nothing of the kind. His method is purely aprioristic. Like Hobbes, 'shut up in his cabinet in the dark', he has no need to study nature; he works everything out in his head. It is a little sum: basic repression plus surplus repression yields a troubled and destructive libido; take away surplus repression and the libido retains only its creative and satisfying elements. The magic word is 'transformation', which is oddly like 'conversion' to religious revivalists of the Puritan tradition. It does not just mean change. It means a total alteration from something thoroughly bad to something thoroughly good. And, of course, this 'transformation' is not an empirical concept at all. It is an intellectual construction, and what it entails depends entirely on the manner in which it is constructed.

Marcuse proclaims his attachment to the dialectical method; and the dialectic, in his use of it, turns out to be a kind of conjurer's hat from which truths can be produced like rabbits: 'When historical content enters into the dialectical concept and determines methodologically its development and function, dialectical thought attains the concreteness which links the structure of thought to that of reality. Logical truth becomes historical truth.'

Fortunately, we are not here concerned with Marcuse as a technical philosopher. Indeed he scarcely attempts to assume this role. He offers, admittedly, a defence of the Hegelian metaphysical style of philosophy against the rival tradition of empiricism and positivism, but his criteria are ideological, rather than philosophical. For example, his main objection to positivism is that it serves the interest of conservatism. 'The protagonists of positivism', he writes, 'took great pains to stress the conservative and affirmative attitude of their philosophy; it induces thought to be satisfied with the facts, to renounce any transgression beyond them, and to bow to the given state of affairs.' Correspondingly, Marcuse praises Hegel for holding that 'the facts in themselves possess no authority', and thus preparing the way for what Marcuse considers a truly critical or negative philosophy.

His objections to contemporary logical positivism and linguistic analysis are equally ideological. He even goes so far as to assert that the current techniques of linguistic analysis 'spread the atmosphere of denunciation and investigation by committee. The intellectual is called on the carpet. What do you mean when you say . . .? Don't you conceal something . . .?' But, alas, this wild thought is all he adds to stock accusations against analytic philosophy of methodical triviality, and therefore need not detain us.

V

The nine years which separate *Eros and Civilisation* from Marcuse's next substantial book mark a decline in his spirits. In *One-Dimensional Man*, published in 1964, he is no longer concerned with the possibility of a non-repressive civilisation, but rather with the repressiveness of existing, and especially American civilisation. Julius Gould reviewed the book in *Encounter* (September 1964), under the title 'The Dialectics of Despair', and Allen Graubard's review in the American Left journal *Dissent* was headed 'One-Dimensional Pessimism'. And it is assuredly a bleak and depressing book; that it has also been a US best-seller may suggest, however, that Americans 'can take it'.

At the heart of this book there lies the belief of Babeuf which I have already mentioned, that 'the political sentiments held by a misled, indoctrinated and ignorant populace are not to be regarded as the people's real will and that the establishment of a "real Republic" involves acting (and writing) against the people, against the majority'. Marcuse in *One-Dimensional Man* sets out to show just how misled, indoctrinated, ignorant and indeed corrupted are the people, the majority, in modern industrialised societies. The only society he describes is America, and although he nowhere distinguishes between industrial society in general and the United States in particular, he may be assumed to consider America to be the archetype of such civilisation, and the model towards which all other industrial societies are moving.

Just as he elsewhere attacks liberalism for betraying its own principles, he here attacks modern democracy as a fraudulent system of popular government, vitiated by the perversion of people's minds, and even their souls, by modern techniques of domination. We are never told precisely who dominates, but there are various vague references to vested interests, the Establishment, the ruling classes and the rich. Domination in the abstract is what is usually complained of. However, domination is seen as a characteristic of all known societies, and Marcuse's particular objection to the modern democratic system is that it makes the people mistake their servitude for liberty, and like it.

Affluence itself has corrupted men. Today 'people recognise themselves in their commodities; they find their soul in their automobile, hi-fi set, split-level home, kitchen equipment'. The very productive apparatus, the goods and services which modern society produces 'sell' or impose the social system on the people:

> 'The means of mass transportation and communication, the commodities of lodging, food and clothing, the irresistible output of the entertainment and information industry carry with them prescribed attitudes and habits, certain intellectual and emotional reactions which bind the consumers more or less pleasantly to the producers and, through the latter, to the whole.' (p. 12.)

In this way, as Marcuse puts it, the spread of the material products of industrialisation to more and more people means that 'the indoctrination they carry ceases to be publicity; it becomes a way of life'.

He is ready to admit that this way of life may seem to be *better* than that which preceded the rise of industrialisation even as the Welfare State may seem to be an improvement on previous arrangements. But Marcuse holds that neither form of betterment is genuine because each diminishes the desire for revolution, each 'militates against qualitative change'. Indeed Marcuse goes so far as to speak of 'those whose life is the hell of the Affluent Society' and he asserts that such people are 'kept in line by a brutality which revives medieval and early modern practices'. He enlarges on this last remark by describing the inhabitants of the Affluent Society as slaves:

> 'The slaves of developed industrial civilisation are sublimated slaves, but they are slaves, for slavery is determined neither by obedience nor by hardness of labour but by the status of being a mere instrument, and the reduction of man to the status of a thing.' (p. 32.)

In the Affluent Society, moreover, liberty itself is made

into 'a perfect instrument of domination'; for the freedom
it affords is no more than free competition at administered
prices, a free press that censors itself, free choice between
brands and gadgets. 'Free election of masters,' he adds, 'does
not abolish the masters and the slaves. Free choice among a
wide variety of goods and services does not signify freedom,
if those goods and services . . . sustain alienation.' As for the
equality of which modern American society at any rate
boasts, it is just as spurious, according to Marcuse, just as
inimical to real equality as its so-called liberty is inimical to
real liberty:

> 'If the worker and his boss enjoy the same television
> programmes and visit the same resort places, if the typist
> is as attractively made-up as the daughter of her employer,
> if the Negro owns a Cadillac, if they all read the same
> newspaper, then this assimilation indicates not the dis-
> appearances of classes, but the extent to which the needs
> and satisfactions that serve the preservation of the Estab-
> lishment are shared by the underlying population.' (p. 8.)

In the 'hell of the Affluent Society' people have lost the
spiritual qualities they possessed in simpler and less prosperous societies, lost even the capacity they had for sexual
experience: 'compare love-making in a meadow and in an
automobile, on a lovers' walk outside the town walls and on
a Manhattan street. In the former cases the environment
partakes of and invites libidinal cathexis and tends to be
eroticised. Libido transcends beyond the immediate eroto-
genic zones – a process of non-repressive sublimation. In
contrast, a mechanised environment seems to block such
self-transcendence of libido.'

To Marcuse the so-called sexual freedom of modern per-
missive society is simply another fraud; it is even worse than
the old taboos because such 'greater liberty involves a
contraction rather than extension and development of instinctual needs . . . it works *for* rather than *against* the *status
quo* of general repression'.

Worst of all, industrial society has killed the urge to resistance. The class war between bourgeoisie and workers has ended not only in 'collusion' between the labour unions and the employers, but in a reconciliation of the workers to their own condition; they are all so well off in their own eyes that they can no longer act as 'agents of historical transformation'. Workers and bourgeois, united by their desire to preserve existing institutions, suffer from the same disease, the Hegelian 'Happy Consciousness', a form of comfortable self-deception about their own true interests; they believe that productivity, industrial output, more and more consumer goods are to everyone's advantage. 'The technological controls appear to be the very embodiment of Reason for the benefit of all social groups and interests – to such an extent that all contradiction seems irrelevant and all counteraction impossible.' Moreover, 'the intellectual and emotional refusal to go along appears neurotic and impotent'. This is the most lamentable feature of the present era: 'the passing of the historical forces which, at the preceding stage of industrial society, seemed to represent the possibility of new forms of existence.'

The corrupted mind of the modern man allows him, Marcuse notes with bitterness, to accept without protest preparations for nuclear war, the falsehoods and vulgarity of advertising, and the built-in obsolescence of automobiles. Intellectuals are as much affected by the process as the rest of society. The *homo conformans* of modern society is a 'one-dimensional man', one who follows 'a pattern of one-dimensional thought and behaviour in which ideas, aspirations and objectives that by their content transcend the established universe of discourse and action are either repelled or reduced to the terms of this universe'. The missing dimension is the dimension of critical awareness or 'negative' thinking.

Language itself is corrupted. Marcuse speaks of the illogicality and ugliness of style in a typical *Time* news item, and contrasts it (somewhat as he contrasts love-making in a meadow and in cars) with the classical literary and logical qualities exhibited by (of all things) *The Communist Manifesto*. The style of modern journalism and publicity has, and seeks to have, a hypnotic effect. Its aim is not communication from mind to mind, but the 'overwhelming' of the reader's consciousness. And in its most sophisticated form, the effect of this hypnotic language is that 'people don't believe it, or don't care and yet act accordingly'. *Homo conformans* is not a fool; he is not deceived by others; his misfortune is that he deceives himself. One-dimensional man is his own creation.

In such a situation, the difference between modern democratic and totalitarian systems diminishes:

'By virtue of the way it has organised its technological base, contemporary industrial society tends to be totalitarian. For "totalitarianism" is not only a terroristic political co-ordination of society, but also a non-terroristic economic technical co-ordination which operates through the manipulation of needs by vested interests. It thus precludes the emergence of an effective opposition against the whole. Not only a specific form of government or party rule makes for totalitarianism, but also a specific system of production and distribution which may well be compatible with a "pluralism" of parties, newspapers, "countervailing powers", etc.' (p. 3.)

Here presumably is another dialectical transformation: as liberalism turns itself into fascism, democracy turns itself into totalitarianism.

VI

What are the prospects of redemption? In *One-Dimensional Man*, Marcuse scarcely considers them. It follows from his diagnosis that modern industrial civilisation is getting worse and not better, and that the same charmless features of the most advanced of modern societies are likely to be reproduced in the others as they catch up. Even so, Marcuse does discern one faint ray of hope, one slender possibility of a revolutionary movement emerging.

On his penultimate page, he writes:

'Underneath the conservative popular base is the substratum of the outcasts and outsiders, the exploited and the persecuted of other races and other colours, the unemployed and the unemployable. They exist outside the democratic process, their life is the most immediate and the most real need for ending intolerable conditions and institutions. Thus their opposition is revolutionary even if their consciousness is not. Their opposition hits the system from without and is therefore not deflected by the system; it is an elementary force that violates the rules of the game. . . . The fact that they start refusing to play the game may be the fact which marks the beginning of the end of a period.' (p. 256.)

Marcuse adds candidly: 'Nothing indicates that it will be a good end.' And his book closes on a mournful note. But since he published *One-Dimensional Man* in 1964 this idea that salvation might come through 'outsiders' has evidently blossomed in his mind. It is, of course, the same idea that Fanon and Sartre and others hold of a 'new proletariat' being constituted by the *damnés de la terre*, the coloured races, 'the victims of neo-colonialism' and such-like to perform the historic revolutionary mission which the prosperous Western working classes have abandoned. This 'New Proletariat' of Outsiders is also one with which *déraciné* intellectuals and students[10] readily identify themselves; for it is a proletariat which is at the same time an *élite*. On Marcuse's analysis it must be one, since the majority is in such a pitiful condition. The 'vast majority accepts, and is made to accept' prevailing values; and does not know the difference between 'true and false consciousness.'

[10] Discussing student protests on BBC television, R. T. McKenzie had this exchange with Marcuse (*Listener*, October 17, 1968): 'I have the uncomfortable feeling that a certain section of the student movement is committed to a wrecking operation.' 'I think that is a minority. I do not identify myself with it, although I would not discard their activities as merely a wrecking operation.' 'Are you arguing there can be no enemy to the left?' 'The left is such that an enemy on the left is rather hard to imagine. We have so many enemies on the right.'

Marcuse's argument is neatly summed up in this paragraph (my italics):

> 'In the last analysis, the question of what is true and false needs to be answered by the individuals themselves, *but only in the last analysis*: that is, if and when they are free to give their own answer. As long as they are kept incapable of being autonomous, as long as they are indoctrinated and manipulated (down to their very instincts) *their answer to this question cannot be taken as their own.*' (p. 6.)

Marcuse's theory of toleration, as set forth in *A Critique of Pure Tolerance*, follows logically from this position. Toleration, as one need hardly say, is regarded as a virtue in all liberal and democratic societies. And Marcuse professes his assent: tolerance *is* a good thing, it is an end in itself. 'The elimination of violence, and the reduction of suppression to the extent required for protecting men and animals from cruelty and aggression are preconditions for the creation of a human society.' But alas, he adds, such a society does not yet exist. In the societies which do exist what is proclaimed and practised as tolerance 'serves the cause of oppression'. Things are tolerated which ought not to be tolerated, and what ought to be tolerated is not tolerated.

Once again Marcuse protests about the hell of the Affluent Society where evil is accepted and even thought to be good so long as it serves the cause of affluence: 'The tolerance of the systematic moronisation of children and adults alike by publicity and propaganda, the release of destructiveness in driving, the recruitment for and training of special forces, the impotent and benevolent tolerance towards outright deception in merchandising, waste and planned obsolescence, are not distortions and aberrations, they are the essence of a system which fosters tolerance as a means for perpetuating the struggle for existence and suppressing the alternative.'

Toleration is historically a progressive idea, Marcuse agrees. But, he asserts, 'within a repressive society even progressive movements can have a reactionary effect if they accept the rules of the game'. For example, he suggests that the exercise of citizens' rights in modern so-called democracies, by voting, writing letters to the press, and taking part in *protest-demonstrations with a prior renunciation of counter-violence* (I shall return to this question of violence later), in effect simply 'serves to strengthen repressive administration' by testifying to the existence of non-existent liberties. It is worth remembering that this proposal that socialists should hold aloof from established politics was one of Bakunin's policies, and one which annoyed Marx exceedingly.

VII

Marcuse believes that the only tolerance worth having is what he calls 'partisan tolerance'. Any kind of impartial or non-partisan tolerance simply 'protects the already established system'. The chief characteristic of partisan tolerance is that it is intolerant towards the 'repressive status quo'. Marcuse adds:

> 'Tolerance cannot be indiscriminate and equal with respect to the contents of expression, neither in word nor deed, it cannot protect false words and wrong deeds which demonstrate that they contradict and counteract the possibilities of liberation. Such indiscriminate tolerance is justified in harmless debates, in conversation, in academic discussion; it is indispensable in scientific enterprise, in private religion. But society cannot be indiscriminate where the pacification of existence, where freedom and happiness themselves are at stake; here, certain policies cannot be proposed, certain behaviour cannot be permitted without making tolerance an instrument for the continuation of servitude.' (p. 88.)

Marcuse recalls that the theory of toleration, as put forward by its most philosophical exponents, is based on the assumption that men are rational creatures, capable of seeing the truth for themselves and of discerning their own rights and interests. Such, Marcuse continues, is 'the rationale of free speech and assembly'. But 'universal tolerance becomes questionable when its rationale no longer prevails, when

tolerance is administered to manipulated and indoctrinated
individuals who parrot, as their own, the opinions of their
masters, for whom heteronomy has become autonomy. . . .'[11]

Precisely because people are thus indoctrinated by the very
conditions under which they live, the only way for them to
be enabled to distinguish the truth is for them to be freed
from this indoctrination. And this, Marcuse does not hesitate
to say, means *counter-indoctrination*.

Here we meet the crucial part of his argument. Marcuse does
not accept the ancient notion that ye shall know the truth
and the truth shall set ye free. Biased information can only be
corrected by information equally biased. Freeing men from
the prevailing indoctrination, Marcuse explains, 'means that
the trend would have to be reversed; they would have to get
their information slanted in the opposite direction. For the
facts are never given immediately and never accessible
immediately; they are established, "mediated" by those
who made them; the truth, "the whole truth", surpasses
these facts and requires the rupture with their appearance.'

Having said this, Marcuse protests that he does not wish
to introduce any dictatorship, but only to replace totalitarian
democracy with a genuinely free society which would not
allow itself to be subverted by a manipulated majority. The
'apparently undemocratic means' – as he calls them – likely
to be necessary to promote such a transformation,

'include the withdrawal of toleration of speech and
assembly from groups and movements which promote

[11] In his BBC television broadcast, Marcuse gave another reason for
favouring 'discriminating tolerance', or 'intolerance towards movements
from the right, intolerance of movements from the right'. Marcuse explained (*Listener*, October 17, 1968):
'You see, I believe that we have the discriminating tolerance today
already, and what I want to do is redress the balance. The Left, and
especially the militant Left, lacks the funds that are necessary to be heard
in the mass media. They have no newspapers of large circulation, they
cannot get any of the larger television networks. So you have a perfectly
legal discriminating tolerance already.'

aggressive policies, armament, chauvinism, discrimination on the grounds of race and religion, or which oppose the extension of public services, social security, medical care, etc. Moreover, the restoration of freedom of thought may necessitate new and rigid restrictions on teachings and practices in the educational institutions which, by their very methods and concepts, serve to enclose the mind within the established universe of discourse and behaviour.'

But who is to articulate and impose these 'rigid restrictions'? Marcuse is disappointingly vague: 'While the reversal of the trend in the educational enterprise could conceivably be enforced by the students and teachers themselves, and thus be self-imposed, the systematic withdrawal of tolerance towards regressive and repressive opinions and movements could only be envisaged as results of large-scale pressure which would amount to an upheaval.'

'Upheaval' is presumably another word for 'revolution'. But what kind of revolution? Again Marcuse cuts off his narrative with these difficult questions unanswered: 'The author is fully aware that, at present, no power, no authority, no government exists which would translate liberating tolerance into practice; but he believes that it is the task and duty of the intellectual to recall and preserve historical possibilities which seem to have become utopian possibilities – that it is his task to break the concreteness of oppression in order to open the mental space in which this society can be recognised as what it is and does.'

The one thing that Marcuse does reveal about the upheaval or revolution he desires is that it entails violence. I have already quoted his condemnation of those who participate 'in protest-demonstrations with a prior renunciation of counter-violence'. Marcuse is frank in his scorn for the belief of Gandhi and Martin Luther King in non-violent resistance.

'To refrain from violence in the face of vastly superior violence is one thing; to renounce *a priori* violence against violence, on ethical or psychological grounds (because it may antagonise sympathisers) is another.' 'Non-violence,' he adds,

is 'a necessity rather than a virtue,' and 'normally it does not
harm the cause of the strong.'

Like Sartre, Marcuse claims that violence is a feature of
all existing regimes. 'Even in the advanced centres of civilisation,' Marcuse writes, 'violence actually prevails.' And
this to his eyes is bad violence. But violence used *against* the
established system is another matter altogether.

> 'In terms of historical function, there is a difference be-
> tween revolutionary and reactionary violence, between
> violence practised by the oppressed and by the oppressors.
> In terms of ethics, both forms of violence are inhuman, and
> evil – but *since when is history made in accordance with ethical
> standards?* To start applying them at the point where the
> oppressed rebel against the oppressors, the have-nots
> against the haves, is serving the cause of actual violence by
> weakening the protest against it.' (p. 103, italics added.)

What Marcuse means by 'actual violence' is that force
which reinforces law in existing societies; and he goes on to
make the bold suggestion that the chances of human progress
seem 'to involve the calculated choice between two forms of
political violence; that on the part of the legally constituted
powers . . . and that on the part of potentially subversive
movements'. He asks: 'Can the historical calculus be reasonably extended to the justification of one form of violence
against another?' There is not much doubt in his answer:

> 'With all the qualifications of a hypothesis based on an
> "open" historical record, it seems that violence emanating
> from the rebellion of the oppressed classes broke the
> historical continuum of injustice, cruelty and silence for a
> brief moment, brief but explosive enough to achieve an
> increase in the scope of freedom and justice and . . .
> progress in civilisation.' (p. 107.)

In short Marcuse holds that so long as violence comes from
below, from the 'oppressed', it is acceptable. And he thinks
history gives him rational grounds for this conclusion. His
conception of what actually happened in history is admittedly odd. Our modern civilisation, he fancies, 'was pain-

fully born in the violence of the heretic revolts of the thir-
teenth century and the peasant and labourer revolts of the
fourteenth century'. But Marcuse's history is less worrying
than the conclusions, the moral conclusions, which he uses
his history to sustain.

VIII

I have been concerned in this essay more to expound Marcuse's theories than to criticise them, although I will confess
that I think that one has only to set forth clearly the main
lines of his thinking to reveal it as being at once nugatory and
dangerous. It is nugatory because it rests on premises
which cannot be justified, and because it is developed by
arguments which serve only to enlarge its defects. It is
dangerous because it advocates intolerance and confers a
blessing on violence. While paying lip-service to reason and
truth, Marcuse appeals continuously to passion and recommends what can only be called the bending of truth to the
service of a revolutionary end.

The analytic devices he introduces are worthless. His distinction, for example, between basic and surplus repression
is no aid to understanding because he gives us no means of
telling what surplus repression is. There is really no room for
discussion here. Nobody believes in surplus repression, because the word 'surplus' means, by definition, that which is
in excess of what is needed. And even a Stalin could say he
did not believe in having any more repression than was
needed, though of course he had different ideas of what was
needed than others might have. Assuredly, Marcuse offers
some explanation of what he himself considers surplus repression, namely that repression which is needed to uphold
'class domination'. But this does not help us, because the
most repressive societies known to history have either been
wholly classless, as in the case of the USSR, or almost classless, as was the Third Reich. The most class-stratified
societies, such as England in the eighteenth century, have
sometimes been the least repressive. Of course, the word

'repression' is itself so loaded, so pejorative, that it sounds odd to speak in favour of any kind of repression at all. And this was one of Freud's misfortunes, that writing in ordinary language, he had to use words that were not scientific or neutral or *wertfrei* as he would have liked them to be, but which had a heavy evaluative content, so to speak, built into them. Freud met this difficulty, not altogether successfully, by developing a quasi-technical vocabulary of his own. Marcuse, by contrast, ignores the difficulty. And as a result his style is a formless mixture of quasi-technical terms and ideological jargon, of rhetoric and of everyday language.

Moreover, in addition to the distinctions that Marcuse makes uselessly, there are the distinctions that he refuses to acknowledge. For example, violence is never distinguished from force. The only difference that Marcuse recognises is that between revolutionary and reactionary violence. He thus banishes the simple, but very important, distinction between the force, or strong arm, seldom actually used, of the law and that aggressive infliction of injury or damage which is violence as the dictionary defines the word. 'Violence' is another word which has an element of censure incorporated in its meaning; 'force' is a word with a distinctively different use; force is not by definition immoderate. And Marcuse's manner of lumping together legitimate force and terrorism in the same category of violence is to make nonsense of the whole conception of the rule of law, which is nevertheless a phrase that he himself employs.

In a similar way, Marcuse's indiscriminate use of the word 'totalitarian', whether for such countries as the Soviet Union or for the United States, robs the word 'totalitarian' of any utility. For quite apart from the relative virtues of Russia and America, their objectively verifiable methods of government are so vastly different that any one word which describes them both equally well is bound to be a word that tells us very little about either.

But what is perhaps the most ruinous defect of Marcuse's whole Anarcho-Marxist theory is that it combines the worst features of both Anarchism and Marxism, with few of the merits of either. This comes out most clearly in the means he recommends to achieve his libertarian ends. For it is not that he proposes, in the manner of Bakunin and the nineteenth-century anarchists, simply to destroy the old system by burning down government buildings and so forth. Such destructive *élan*, however lamentable it may be in moral terms, is not inconsistent with a demand for the abolition of all government. But Marcuse asks for more than this. He calls not only for terror, but for a reign of terror. He asks for the suppression of conservatives, for the suppression of conservative speech, even of conservative thought. This requires the creation of institutions of suppression which must exist for as long as conservative thoughts are likely to continue to exist in anyone's mind. Marcuse is therefore calling for something uncannily like the State-that-is-to-wither-away (but not wither away very soon) which is at once the most conspicuous and the most charmless feature of Communist Party ideology. For all his attacks on Stalinism, Marcuse himself is advocating the very things that make Stalinism odious. And let us not be led astray by Marcuse's constant avowal of his attachment to the idea of freedom; as Milton and Locke remarked in the seventeenth century, the people who talk most about liberty are frequently its greatest enemies.

IX

In seeking to distinguish the main lines of his argument and the principle of coherence which unifies his work, I have withheld attention from one feature which ought not to be neglected. Marcuse presents himself so determinedly as a Hegelian rationalist, he goes on and on so much about reason, that one almost forgets to remark how much he is a man of feeling. *Eros and Civilisation* is a highly romantic work. The best chapters are those devoted to poetry and aesthetics, where the author speaks of the need for 'the self-sublimation of sensuousness' as the way to creation of a free culture, the same idea that was advanced with such valiant repetitiveness by the late Sir Herbert Read, who recognised that it belonged to romanticism and not to rationalism. Marcuse writes with a remarkable sympathy about Schiller, Rilke and Baudelaire; in the world of literature and mythology, he is clearly at ease and at home.

This is not to say that he gives the impression of exercising to a marked degree the faculty of imagination. In all his strictures on the Affluent Society and the welfare state, he never enters for one moment the mind of the working man in the real world, to whom the dawn of prosperity after years of unemployment and recession meant an immense step forward from woeful deprivation to a decent condition of life; or the minds of those afflicted and needy people to whom the welfare state has brought such signal relief. To Marcuse the past means making love in meadows in an age when a gentlemanly life was still possible. His attitude to the present world is often indistinguishable from that of any elderly Blimp or Junker:

The degree to which the population is allowed to break the peace wherever there is still peace and silence, to be ugly and uglify things, to ooze familiarity, to offend against good form is frightening. It is frightening because it expresses the lawful and even organised effort to reject the Other in his own right, to prevent autonomy even in a small, reserved sphere of existence. In the over-developed countries, an ever-larger part of the population becomes one huge captive audience – captured not by a totalitarian régime, but by the liberties of the citizens whose media of amusement and elevation compel the Other to partake of their sounds, sights and smells. (p. 245.)

I have put this paragraph in italics because I conceive it to be the key passage not only to *One-Dimensional Man*, but to Marcuse's whole attitude. He often uses the word *alienation*. Alienation is the central theme of the Marxism he expounded as long ago as 1941 in *Reason and Revolution*; he might even claim with Georg Lukács the honour of having introduced the word into Left-wing conversation. But it is also a word that can be aptly applied to Marcuse's own predicament. His feelings about the real world, towards the 'repressive civilisation' which is the only kind of civilisation we know, towards 'domination', which is the only kind of political order we have, are manifestly alienated. Far more than his divine discontent and moral disapproval towards the inhabitants of the modern world, one is conscious of a simple disgust. The people, the populace, the majority, are manipulated, indoctrinated, enslaved; Marcuse cannot bear their sights, their sounds, their smells.

And here, of course, he is very unlike Bakunin, the Russian nobleman who adored the simple people, and detected in the honest sweat of labourers the true scent of human excellence. Marcuse has more German instincts, recoiling from the *Untermenschen*. In an interview in Venice given to an Italian magazine Marcuse said that Venice ought to be reserved for high-class tourism only (*un turismo di qualità*), and that the *hoi polloi* who disturbed its solemn beauty should be kept out (*Il Tempo*, August 1968, p. 17). The idea of mankind appeals to him; real men – most of them – sicken him. For this reason it is as difficult to believe in his anarchism as it is, for other reasons, to believe in his Marxism. Marcuse's 'negative philosophy' is assuredly negative; his 'negations' are real negations, and not in the fanciful sense for which he claims the authority of Hegel, but in the ordinary sense of rejection or denial of the positive. Ideologists march, like soldiers, on their stomachs; and Marcuse has the stomach of a very high-class aesthete, queasy, fastidious and misanthropic.

FRANTZ FANON

Aristide R. Zolberg

FRANTZ FANON

Aristide R. Zolberg

I

The problems of independence in Africa have generated a
new literature of philosophy, ideology and theory which reflects, beneath a certain amount of cant, a serious appreciation of the solemnity of political foundations. Beyond its
appeal for a specialised audience, the political drama that is
being enacted also offers a bonus to the amateur of repertory
revival. In spite of many efforts to devise original formu-
lations, African political thought continues to be cast in
moulds designed in Europe. Committed to a democratic
legitimacy but persuaded that they alone are qualified to
rule, many of Africa's insecure oligarchs have been putting
forward theories that stress 'the general will' as expressed
through the rulers of a 'monolithic party'. The exceptions to
this Jacobin trend, and the reactions it has engendered, also
have an uncanny familiar sound. The struggle of the opposition in Ghana bore a striking resemblance to that of the
Fédérés; the Nigerians speak the language of Burke or of
Madison; and in the Ivory Coast Houphouet-Boigny's
régime, based on government rather than on party and intent on creating an indigenous bourgeoisie, might well be
summed up in another echo: *Enrichissez-vous.* . . .

Will the high tide of political messianism which arose in
Europe after the abortive first classic revolution also engulf
Africa? Religious movements with political overtones have
been endemic to many parts of the continent. Where de-
colonisation was relatively easy and rapid, however, such
movements tended to be submerged by Congress-type organisations led by educated men who had little cause for despair
and among whom the utopian spirit was seldom manifest.
More recently, however, it has become obvious that the

usual nationalist strategies are of little use in areas where intractable white minorities refuse to negotiate. Furthermore, in the new states themselves, many Africans have begun to agree with the observers who say that the continent is off to a bad start. Independence has fostered great expectations, an acute awareness of the immense obstacles that prevent their fulfilment, and a growing impatience with the incumbent rulers who have a limited understanding of what is to be done. Few among the opposition wish for a Restoration. But many believe that the 'new class' and the 'bureaucratic bourgeoisie' are fundamentally corrupt. The true revolution – the revolution that will constitute a new beginning – is yet to come.

Its prophet has already appeared. Like his European predecessors, Frantz Fanon has conjured up a Manichean world in which the colonised, a world-wide proletariat, are the damned. His gospel, *Les Damnés de la terre*, was written during the last year of his brief life and published about a month before he died of leukaemia in October, 1961, at the age of thirty-six.[1] It is the last act of a decade of public life during which its author joined to the career of the physician-scholar that of political militant; to a love of French culture hatred of French colonial policy; to a belief in universal values the aspirations of colonial nationalists; to the world of the coloniser the world of the colonised. Born in Martinique as a French citizen, he had become Algerian by choice and was serving the Provisional Government of the Algerian Republic as its ambassador in Accra when his health began to falter in mid-1960. The last year of his life appears like a desperate attempt to span the world: to Tunis to rest; to the USSR in the vain hope of effective medical care; to Rome, for a last encounter with the world of the

[1] Frantz Fanon, *Les Damnés de la terre* (Paris). François Maspero, 1961: 'Cahiers Libres', Nos. 27–28. An English edition, *The Damned*, was published by Présence Africaine (Paris, 1964). The same text has appeared in England and the United States as *The Wretched of the Earth* (New York: Grove Press; London: MacGibbon & Kee and Penguin).

left-bank now closed to him; and finally to a last hospital in Washington, D.C., where, as he lay dying, he believed himself to be like Lumumba, at the mercy of his murderous enemies.[2] His grave in Algeria was his first resting-place since his departure from the Antilles at the end of World War II.

II

Frantz Fanon was a Negro and a psychiatrist. These are essential facts in the career of the political thinker which began with the publication in 1952 of *Peau Noire, Masques Blancs*, in the Editions du Seuil. Before World War II, educated Martiniquais knew no culture other than that of France, no identity other than a French identity. Like a European child who discovered in the midst of Nazi persecutions that he was a Jew, Fanon, the dark-skinned Frenchman, discovered that he was a 'Nigger' when the delicate balance of Martinique was upset by the sudden influx of 10,000 refugee French sailors during World War II. Blackness pursued him when, as a youth, he joined the First French Army towards the end of the war, and afterwards, while he studied medicine in Lyons. This unresolved crisis of identity in himself and others was the obsession that propelled his thought. What started out as a medical thesis on the relevance of classical psychoanalysis to the psycho-pathology of the Negro in a white world became his first book.

The psycho-analytic materials scattered through Fanon's work are often commonplace and simplistic; reports of therapy with which he closes *Les Damnés de la terre* are as improbable as miraculous; and there is no evidence as to whether he had many cures to his credit. But from the very beginning he displayed a brilliant knack for transforming clinical insights into political poetry designed to achieve his fundamental purpose. In an early article discussing North African patients in a French hospital, he pointed out that there is a 'North African syndrome' of which individual

---

[2] The circumstances of his death and several conversations are related by Simone de Beauvoir in *La Force des Choses* (Paris, Gallimard, 1963).

illnesses are but a manifestation; the solution must therefore be sought in the social situation internalised by individuals.[3] Similarly he reasoned that neuroses exist among West Indians even where there is no evidence of personal trauma; hence they must stem from the status of the entire group. Fanon therefore undertook to invent the collective therapy required to save a race.

Using materials familiar to readers of the American psycho-analytic sociology of race-relations of just before the Second World War – but which he seems to have known only through its literary expression in Richard Wright and others – he sought to demonstrate in *Peau Noire* that Negrophobia arises from the sexual repression Europeans underwent in the process of striving for high achievement. Blackness comes to be identified with dangerous instincts, with sin, with evil. As such it finds its place in the collective unconscious – not of 'man', as Fanon argues in a sally against Jung – but of 'the European'. In fundamental contrast, the black man, personified by the French-speaking West Indian, has no Oedipus complex. Sexual deviations of any sort are unknown to him (transvestites, whom Fanon has observed in Martinique, are dismissed by him as playful masqueraders). The psychic tragedy of the Negro is that he has assimilated the European collective unconscious along with a European language and culture. Sartre's dialectical dictum provides Fanon with a major lead: as the anti-Semite creates the Jew, so the Negrophobe creates the Nigger. Now, wherever he may be, whatever else he may be, the Nigger is not a man, he is a black man, who fears and hates his blackness.

There follows a desperate search for escape, but all paths lead to dead-ends. The Nigger wishes to disappear, but can do so only in his dreams. He learns to speak French and fancies himself becoming whiter, more of a man. But this white mask is a false *persona*, incompatible with reality. The more he tries to become a European, the more he is made

[3] *Pour la Révolution Africaine* (Paris, F. Maspero, 1964) 'Cahiers Libres', Nos. 53–4. The essay appeared originally in *Esprit*, 1952.

aware of his blackness. If he becomes a doctor, his patients
will say 'We have a Negro doctor: his hands are very gentle.'
If he becomes a professor, the students will whisper, 'We
have a Negro professor, he is very intelligent.' Finally, to the
white in love with whiteness, the Nigger attempts to oppose
his own narcissism. Like many other French-speaking intellectuals, Fanon had followed the lead of his countryman, the
poet Aimé Césaire, into a contemplation of 'the glorious
humility of a race that had never accomplished anything...'.
The word had become flesh through the founding of *Présence
Africaine* in Paris in 1947. But the following year, in a preface
to Léopold Senghor's *Anthologie de la nouvelle poésie nègre et
malgache*, Sartre raised this Black Orpheus only to subject him
to a cruel indictment: his *négritude* is an 'anti-racist racism',
which can be but a 'negative moment' that reinforces the
fundamental division of the world and must bow to in-
exorable dialectical progress. Fanon raged at his fiendish
master but submitted to his logic. He concluded that the only
hope for effective cure lies in commitment, in the existentialist praxis. The black man will not be a man until he is
recognised as a man by other men; he will remain enslaved
until he has successfully struggled for his political freedom.

The solution itself is hardly original. What distinguishes
Fanon, however, is that he believed that the black masses
needed a myth without which, as Sorel said in his *Reflections
on Violence*, 'one may go on talking revolt indefinitely without
ever provoking any revolutionary movement'. Although he
does not yet provide it in *Peau Noire*, the accents of utopia are
already present. In his account of the psycho-dynamics of
colonisation, he implies that at the beginning there was a
state of psychic peace, but this was violated by the Europeans,
who are themselves the victims of history. In the end, however, the Manichean world will be a community once again;
the state of innocence will be reinstated. It is the elaboration
of this myth which provides the main theme for the decade
that followed.

III

A year after the publication of this book, Fanon was in Algeria where as a French physician, albeit black, his status was superior to that of North African Muslims, in whose eyes he was an inferior man of the Sudan. Within a year of his arrival, the Algerian rising had begun. As head of the psychiatric service of the administrative hospital of Blida-Joinville, Fanon led a double life for nearly two years. He cared for French victims of Algerian terror and trained Muslim saboteurs. He comforted a policeman exhausted from a demanding daily routine which included questioning Algerians under torture, but also pieced together victims of his patient's zeal. In 1956, the man who had stated that writing was for him a form of meditation, a prelude to action, made his choice: with a letter to the Minister-Resident baring the struggle of his soul, he resigned his post and prepared to join the revolution.

The experiences of these years were fundamental. Confronted with the Algerian situation, Fanon altered his vision: he no longer saw a world divided into Black and White, but into Coloniser and Colonised. In an address on 'Racism and Culture' which he delivered before the first Congress of Negro Writers and Artists (held in Paris in September, 1956), he argued that racism is not an independent phenomenon but rather 'the most visible element' of a total hierarchical relationship established by a group endowed with a technical advantage over another. In order to consolidate their hold, the colonisers must destroy the cultural system of the colonised. Deprived of their values, the latter become manipulatable objects which can then be assimilated into the new order; what was a life-giving indigenous culture becomes a mummy which imprisons the colonised in a stultified traditionalism; apathy, inertia, an inferiority complex, guilt, follow. Racism must therefore be viewed not as something innate in man or as a 'psychological flaw', but as a necessary ideological weapon which accompanies domination. Even if, like France, it prides itself on universalism, a colonial country *must* be racist. Nevertheless, since such a weapon must be flexible in order to retain its effectiveness, it undergoes many metamorphoses. Having been forced to abandon a more primitive version based on biological attributes, the dominant group invents a new ethnocentric hierarchy of ways of life; when this too comes under fire, racism is treated as an unfortunate aberration and a committee of the United Nations is formed to eradicate it. But Fanon warns against this new economism: 'the superstructure of exploitation' will disappear only through a struggle for political liberation.

It is in relation to the nature of this struggle that Fanon's thought underwent a second transformation during these Algerian years. The sensitive man, the healer, recoiled from the horrors of war, and particularly from the mental breakdowns it caused on both sides; but the ideologue was mesmerised by the 'creative power of revolution', by the 'purifying flame of violence'. After a brief trip to France he rejoined the Algerian leadership in Tunis and undertook two assignments which involved these two selves: the healer worked in the Algerian army's field hospitals, while the ideologue became an editorial writer for *El Moujahid*, central organ of the FLN. Fanon's vision grew sharper, and he affirmed in the concluding sentence of his second book his faith in the myth that was to save the colonised:

> The Revolution in depth, the true revolution because it transforms man and renews society, is very advanced. This oxygen which invents and organises a new humanity, it is that also, the Algerian Revolution.[4]

In the orgy of self-hatred that serves as a preface to *Les Damnés*, Sartre claims that Fanon, 'if you neglect the fascistic chatter of Sorel, is the first since Engels to have turned the spotlight on the midwife of history'. But *L'An V de la Révolution Algérienne* is inconceivable without Sorel – although I do not believe that Fanon ever refers to this predecessor in any of his works. Most of the book is devoted to a demonstration

[4] *L'An V de la Révolution Algérienne* (Paris, F. Maspero, 1959), 'Cahiers Libres', No. 3.

of the therapeutic effects of participation in the revolution on man and society. In an extraordinary analysis of the symbol of the Veil, Fanon illustrates how this process takes place. He initially interprets European attempts to modernise Algeria by improving the status of women as a disguised form of aggressiveness: the will to remove the veil means rape, but rape itself is but a personalisation of the desire to subjugate the entire society. Hence, for the Algerians, the wearing of the veil became a major symbol of resistance; through it, tradition was exalted; thus, Algeria too produced its *négritude*. But following the usual dialectical reasoning, such a reaction is regressive: in the process of enhancing tradition, the Algerians became its prisoners. Liberation came with revolution. When women began to function as spies in the European city, sometimes even acting as prostitutes in order to do so, they also shed the veil. Although as the revolution grew they resumed the wearing of it because of its usefulness in carrying hidden weapons and explosives, the veil had now become camouflage. It is no longer part of the enforced identity of the Algerian woman, but results from a choice. By engaging in violence she has become fully human.

More fundamental in its effects than mere nationalist strikes, boycotts or demonstrations, the armed insurrection of the Algerian people is 'the great shock which founds a new world'. As a 'total praxis', combat can bring about the total transformation of a colonial dependency into a renovated community free of any psychological, emotional or legal subjection, within which the colonised will be men. Just as for Sorel the proletariat asserts its existence in the general strike, for Fanon the colonised masses become transfigured through the single combat. Furthermore, as for Sorel the general strike also prepared the proletariat for its post-revolutionary task, so with the Algerian revolution. Fanon argues that the entire structure of the Algerian family undergoes a 'mutation'. Relationships between parents and children, elder and younger brothers, husbands and wives, lose their restrictive traditional character. The revolution even transforms basic attitudes towards technology. Muslims who viewed the radio as an 'evil voice', disruptive of the moral order, now anxiously listen to the voice of the army of liberation; Arabic loses its religious exclusivism, the French language becomes domesticated; a new national *logos* is being created. Peasants, suspicious of modern medicine, become soldiers who rapidly understand the value of inoculations and of personal hygiene; medicine is accepted because it has become a revolutionary weapon; it is the end of superstition. Violence creates a new spiritual unity which prepares tne country for the immense task of national reconstruction after the war. The nation is consecrated in blood. Through violence, the Manichean world will be set right again.

IV

For whom was Fanon forging this frightful myth? Where could the prophet find a people in need of salvation? Simone de Beauvoir writes of his passionate desire to find roots in Algeria; 'but the difficulty was that, among the leaders, no individual or group represented him fully'. He remained an outsider, a black man of the Sudan. And it is naturally to the land of the blacks that he turned during the last years of his life. His aim was clear as early as 1958 when, as one of the Algerian emissaries to the All-African Peoples Conference in Accra, he proposed a revolutionary link between the two Africas through the creation of an African Legion. Although this was in sharp contrast to the non-violent approach favoured by the leaders of established nationalist parties in tropical Africa, he did not give up. After suffering severe wounds when his jeep hit a land-mine on the Moroccan border and barely escaping an attempted assassination attributed to the 'Red Hand' while recovering in Rome, he returned to Accra in 1960 as the Algerian ambassador. While the new rulers exchanged diplomatic niceties at Pan-African cocktail parties, Fanon organised FLN aid for Roberto Holden's Angolan guerrillas and led a mission to northern Mali, beyond Timbuktu, where he hoped to establish a southern base for the FLN through which black African troops could be channelled, perhaps to compensate for the use of such troops by the French in their colonial wars.

Like Richard Wright, the pilgrim had returned to the land of his ancestors. Like Wright, his reaction to it was one of frustrated anger. The year 1960 was that of independence for all the members of the French Community. This, for Fanon and for many Africans, was a fake independence, granted by France to nationalist leaders who remained her clients; they viewed Senghor and Houphouet-Boigny much as uncompromising syndicalists once came to see Jean Jaurès. The break-up of the Mali federation between French Sudan and Senegal was widely interpreted as an indication of the evil power of 'neo-colonialism'. But 1960 was also the year of the Congo. In Lumumba, Fanon saw perhaps the embodiment of a revolutionary ideal he could not find elsewhere on the continent; and although he criticised Lumumba's policies (especially his initial trust in the United Nations), he clearly identified himself with this son of Africa who led a people and became a martyr and lived to witness the Congo's collapse into tribal conflict, the disintegration of a country into a Hobbesian state of nature. In the midst of independence celebrations Fanon saw prophetically that independence did not constitute a new beginning; the one chance for salvation was being dissipated forever.

The reluctance of the new African nations to assume the burden of their revolutionary duty stemmed, he believed, from a lack of understanding of the fundamental nature of the political world. The African élites had no ideological key beyond a commonplace nationalism. In the agony of his last year Fanon willed them the gnosis he had discovered in Algeria, expanded to encompass the whole world and raised to a surrealistic and poetic plane. The French title of his book *Les Damnés de la terre*, taken from the first line of the *Internationale*, is more evocative than its English translation. The wretched elicit our pity, but the damned are beyond hope. The lot of the wretched can be improved by a hand-out, but the damned must be born again. In Fanon's hallucinatory imagery, which links him with Rimbaud and Jean Genet, the damned are the rat pack, the *lumpenproletariat*, the prostitutes and pimps, the brutal peasants, who invade the city through the sewers. The city goes up in flames. The damned are purified in its fire; they are beautiful and holy.

In the first part of the book, an essay 'On Violence', Fanon argues that whatever the formula or the arrangements, 'de-colonisation is always a violent phenomenon'. The discrepancy between this statement and the actual historical record in Africa provides a significant clue to the tone of the entire work. It is not concerned with providing an empirical description or a sociological explanation of political phenomena, but with shaping reality in accordance with 'historical necessity' before it is too late. For Fanon de-colonisation is not merely the establishment of a New State or the achievement of Sovereignty but the replacement of one species of man by another species of man. The world is turned upside down, the last become the first. But this 'programme of absolute disorder' cannot result from the touch of a magic wand or from a natural cataclysm. The colonised peoples must will it by a commitment to fundamental change at any cost and with every means, 'including, of course, violence'. In the Manichean world created by Europe, de-colonisation thus stems from a 'decisive and murderous confrontation of the two protagonists' in the process of which the colonised 'thing' becomes a man, transforms his being from an 'oppressed spectator' into a 'privileged actor, caught in a quasi-grandiose manner by the searchlights of History.'

The thesis proceeds in Fanon's usual manner, combining a psycho-analytic tradition with a Marxist one, but a Marx whom he does not hesitate to 'stretch' in order to encompass a colonial world where the relations of production are themselves a superstructure rooted in the relations of colonialism, and an Engels whose reasoning concerning force can be characterised as 'childish'. In the beginning colonisation is imposed through violence. The violent reaction it generates among the colonised is turned inward, taking the form of muscular tension, heightened criminality within their own community, tribal wars. An unstable equilibrium is achieved through wild dreams, orgiastic religion, frightful myths, dance, possession. Salvation lies in the redirection of this internalised, self-destructive aggressiveness, on to apposite external objects, the utilisation of this energy for a destruction which purges and purifies. The most powerful reservoir of violence is not to be found in the cities, themselves artificial creatures of colonialism, but in the peasantry. 'It alone is revolutionary. It has nothing to lose and everything to gain. . . .' Once set in motion, it will savagely sweep everything before it, making the temptation to compromise disappear. The inflammation of the countryside is the best way to purge the people of the effects of colonisation. Lest it spend itself uselessly through 'blind voluntarism', however, the violent potential of the people must be channelled by a vanguard which understands its use.

V

In the characteristic manner of Utopian thought, Fanon argues that the revolution must be made but also that its triumph is inevitable. Transfiguration occurs only if the entire community chooses the path of 'royal meditation', of 'absolute praxis'; but he reassures his audience that there is little to fear because the colonial powers, constrained by the fundamentally economic character of colonisation cannot afford the one strategy that could defeat the colonised, permanent military occupation. Furthermore, Africans are not alone: violence in one part of the colonial world has consequences in the rest; Dien Bien Phu and Algeria contribute to the liberation of tropical Africa. The major threat of failure, then, does not stem from the danger of European retribution but from the tragic flaw in the character of the intellectuals of the colonies. It is for them that Fanon reserves his harshest condemnation; it is to them that he addresses a desperate plea to share his vision.

Here also Fanon is unwittingly in the mainstream of the

European tradition of what has been called 'the self-hatred of left-wing intellectuals' (and of which there was perhaps no better example than Sorel). The intellectuals who led nationalist movements are, for Fanon, creatures of colonialism who constitute 'a sort of class of individually liberated slaves' yearning to multiply their numbers. At the beginning they contributed to the creation of a useful 'atmosphere of violence', but they rested on their laurels – much as Sorel suggested that 'a cunningly conducted agitation is extremely useful to Parliamentary Socialists, who boast before the Government and the rich middle class of their ability to moderate revolution'. The people must be vaccinated against infection. As the general strike instils in the proletariat habits of liberty, without which the socialist successor state would only benefit the managers, so for Fanon revolution not only transforms colonised man into man, but it 'lifts the people to the level of the leader', ensuring that henceforth 'the demagogues, the opportunists, the magicians will be faced with an impossible task'. At a time when most leaders were busily constructing a doctrine of the One-Party State (which was so often endorsed by friends of Africa abroad as a necessary condition for modernisation), Fanon supplied a savage prophetic indictment of the doctrine and its authors.

Addressing himself to the plausible Marxist argument that 'bourgeois nationalism' constitutes a necessary dialectical phase, he demonstrates that in underdeveloped countries even the bourgeoisie is underdeveloped. It cannot possibly perform the historic role assigned to it by orthodox Marxists because it is not economically creative. The One-Party State is nothing but a dictatorship of this useless bourgeoisie for its own enrichment. The charismatic leader, whose popularity rapidly declines after independence when the masses discover that nothing has changed, is merely 'the director-general of a society of impatient profiteers'. Such a system, which widens the gap between the rulers and the ruled, creates a vacuum which can rapidly be filled by indigenous military

groups or lead to tribal wars and could easily leave the
country at the mercy of a colonial counter-offensive. The
flaw in the system is partly organisational: nationalist parties
are monstrous urban heads without limbs or bodies. If true
integration is to occur, the leaders must rejoin the masses,
live in the country, transform the villages, create party wings
that are not empty shells. Similarly, he prescribes that after
independence, the new economy must be based on co-
operatives in order to avoid corrupting bureaucratisation.
Unless the masses are politicised, this programme cannot be
carried out and there would be only 'a minimal readaptation,
a few reforms at the top, a flag, and far below, the undivided
mass, as medieval as ever, continuing its perpetual slow
motion . . .'.

But none of this is possible without ideology. The intellectuals must go beyond Marx and Freud, beyond Césaire,
Senghor or Nkrumah. They must follow Fanon's lead, abandon their fastidious pursuit of *négritude* and throw themselves
furiously into the task of creating a *littérature engagée*. They
must join him in telling the masses not that the millennium
is at hand, not that they must trust their leaders, but that the
building of a new world can result only from the effort of
all. They must

> make the masses understand that everything depends on
> them, that if we stagnate, it is their fault, and if we ad-
> vance, it is also their fault, that there is no demiurge, that
> there is no famous man, responsible for everything, but
> that the demiurge is the people and that the magic hands
> are in the end only the hands of the people.

In his final exhortation, he urges the intellectuals to cease
imitating and to create. 'Let us leave Europe,' he shouts.
The European model has led nowhere, except to the creation
of a second Europe more monstrous even than the first.
'Don't talk production,' but do not seek a return to nature.
Do not talk 'rhythm'. Look elsewhere for models if you
must. But the fundamental task is to invent, to discover; to
create a new man, a total man. Not only for Africa but for

the sake of Europe as well. Paralleling Sorel to the very end, Fanon wills to the damned the burden of saving mankind.

VI

Murderous humanism, a particular current in the mainstream of political messianism, exposes the paradox of revolutionary intellectuals in old and new nations. As it appears in ideology, 'violence' is a more terrifying phenomenon than it is for the unthinking who merely practise it as an *ad hoc* instrument. At the same time, however, intellectuals preserve their sensitivity – and seek to avoid responsibility for widows and orphans – by distinguishing between their *noble* violence and the base brutality of others. Sorel ingeniously opposed 'force', an instrument of bourgeois oppression, to 'violence', an instrument of proletarian liberation. Although Fanon does not draw this particular contrast, he does surround his concept of violence with a great deal of ambiguity. He dodges responsibility for possible unpleasant consequences by putting the blame for its use on the other side: the need for violence in the struggle for national liberation is a function of the size of resident white minorities and of its use by the colonial power in maintaining hegemony. What sorts of political act would bring about ritual purification is never made explicit. In a discussion of 'non-violence', Fanon dismisses the latter as a mere bargaining, willingness to compromise. But while a section of the book sub-titled 'Of Violence in the International Context' might lead us to expect a discussion of war, we find him merely arguing that the underdeveloped nations must demand aid as a right and back up this demand with the threat of closing their markets to Europe. It would thus seem that 'violence' encompasses almost the entire range of political pressure. Furthermore, as Sorel suggested that 'it is possible . . . to conceive Socialism as being perfectly revolutionary, although there may be only a few short conflicts', so Fanon explains that while in some situations there is no alternative to armed struggle, elsewhere the struggle may be symbolic only and de-colonisation will be rapid. Having witnessed the horrors of Algeria, perhaps he hoped that such would be the case. By stressing 'commitment' rather than consummation of the act, he appears to be exorcising violence as an evil to be feared most while securing the miracle of regeneration.

Why is a miracle needed? Utopian solutions stem from a fundamental lack of confidence in the ability of an oppressed group to manipulate its environment in order to achieve desired goals. Hence, the attempt to create a political magic. Ultimately, Fanon's solution does not differ from the one he had detected ten years earlier in the dreams of black men who sought to become white or to disappear. He has not freed himself from the White Mask and still believes that the blacks *are* less than men. Terrorism and murder are necessary because unless European institutions are totally destroyed they will prevail and corrupt the new world. Fanon's entire work culminates in the pathetic reassurance of a final vision; the New States stand defiant like 'proud and naked adolescents', pure and with life before them, facing a senescent, rotten Europe, rendered impotent by the consequences of a dissolute life. The magician has performed his trick. They are powerful, as others are weak.

VII

Fanon's allotted span was short. Unlike Lenin, he never reached his 'Finland Station'. He escaped the unkind fate of many political prophets by dying before becoming involved in interminable controversies and sectarian splits, and he survives as a legend whom Sartre has canonised in a joint ceremony with Lumumba.[5] His gospel is now beginning to draw world-wide attention. The French edition of *Les Damnés* has sold over 20,000 copies and *Présence Africaine* initiated its translation into English; his earlier works are being reprinted and translated as well; François Maspero

[5] In a preface to *La Pensée Politique de Patrice Lumumba* (Brussels, *Le Livre Africain*, 1963).

has collected his lesser essays into a posthumous book. Although his name does not appear in a listing of 'formative writers' cited by African students in France in 1961, the author of the survey – conducted just before the publication of *Les Damnés* – already quoted him.[6] There is little doubt that if the survey were repeated today Frantz Fanon would appear alongside Victor Hugo, V. I. Lenin and J.-J. Rousseau. It is said that Ben Bella's 1963 reforms were inspired by Fanon and a recent writer on the Congo has drawn attention to the similarity between the prescriptions for violence contained in *Les Damnés* and the tactics of the new insurgents in the Eastern provinces; an American publisher advertising *The Wretched of the Earth* has claimed that the book has 'already influenced' the civil rights movement. Within an amazingly short time, Fanon has acquired the stature of a latter-day prophet.

As was the case with the messianic thinkers of the nineteenth century, Fanon's place in political history will depend less on the intrinsic intellectual merits of his works than on its contributions to the creation of a political mood and its emotional association with particular movements. Although his programme is vague and his doctrine incomplete, some of his prophecies concerning post-independence Africa have already come to pass and the explanations he provides for the prevailing characteristics of the new régimes articulate the beliefs of the frustrated 'successor generation' who have found, upon returning from their studies abroad, that their predecessors have created a world in their own image and that there is no room at the top. Nowhere in Africa can the young intellectuals find a régime which embodies revolutionary virtue. Sékou Touré, who, when Fanon wrote, was youth's leading hope, is now condemned as 'the architect of neo-colonialism' in Guinée. The downfall of Ben Bella has probably contributed to their growing despair. Constrained within the rigid framework of the one-party state they are

[6] Jean-Pierre N'Diaye, *Enquête sur les étudiants noirs en France* (Paris, Editions Réalités Africaines, 1962).

becoming prey to a separatist mood and to a maximalist dream. In search of allies who can provide the mass support required to revive the revolution, the educated youth encounter the youth of the countryside which has already begun its metamorphosis into the immense *Lumpenproletariat* of the growing cities. Demography is on the side of movements based on youth: adolescents and young adults constitute the majority of the population of the new states. The desperate search for salvation leads them beyond the Left to the Final Revolution, the ultimate, endless, contentless consummation of a world where Fanon's ghost awaits them.

Although, so far, more plots have failed than succeeded, Fanon correctly diagnosed the inherent weakness of régimes based on sprawling nationalist movements; a few blows of the axe can bring them down. What hope, then, for the revolution? Rulers will change, their rhetoric will differ, their emissaries will travel to other capitals. At home, however, the most likely outcome will be 'more of the same': a régime with flimsy structures of authority, ill-equipped to cope with the immense task of modernisation, hiding beneath a ritualistic authoritarian facade, and devoting much of its skimpy resources to the maintenance of an oligarchy. Perhaps new spokesmen are coming who will invoke Fanon as the prophet of the Second Revolution. In the end, however, it is likely that his fiercely humanistic spirit will also be consumed in a final tragic irony.

BLACK POWER

George Feaver

BLACK POWER

George Feaver

I

It was a Sunday afternoon in early June, 1966, when James Meredith, whose enrolment as the first Negro at the University of Mississippi was secured in 1962 by a substantial contingent of United States marshals and soldiers, set out alone to walk the 220 miles from Memphis, Tennessee, to Jackson, Mississippi. As he explained to journalists, he hoped by his example to encourage others of his race 'to overcome that all-pervasive and over-riding fear that dominates the day-to-day life of the Negro in the United States'. As news of his intended march spread through the black community (at least according to the grim retrospective humour of Julius Lester's *Look Out Whitey!, Black Power's Gon' Get Your Mama!*), hustlers tried to take out insurance policies on Meredith's life, naming themselves as beneficiaries, Negro ministers distractedly thumbed through their files for old sermons about martyrdom, and florists discreetly placed extra orders for funeral wreaths. True to expectations, Meredith had not penetrated more than ten miles into Mississippi when one Aubrey James Norvell calmly stepped from behind some bushes by the roadside, and, in the bizarre fashion of ethnic conflict in America, cut the lone marcher down with three rounds from his shotgun.

Fortunately, Meredith was not killed. After a brief recuperative period he was, in fact, able to complete his journey to Jackson. By that time, however, his individual act of heroism had been eclipsed by more momentous events. The isolated shooting incident seemed to have precipitated a major new development of emphasis in the long struggle for racial equality in America. Indeed, the last rites of the 'civil rights' phase of the movement had been symbolically pronounced, so far as the impatient younger black leaders were concerned, by the blast of Norvell's ill-aimed weapon.

Already in the corridors of the Memphis hospital where Meredith was taken after the shooting, a fundamental split in tactics was developing among spokesmen for the established rights organisations. The younger blacks, represented by the leadership of SNCC and CORE, called for 'a massive public indictment of the failure of American society, the Government of the United States, and the State of Mississippi' to come to grips with the pervasive 'racism' reflected in senseless attacks upon members of their race. A radical 'Manifesto' was drawn up under the aegis of a caucus of younger militants, to announce a mass march over Meredith's proposed route. Martin Luther King Jr, speaking for the Southern Christian Leadership Conference, warned against framing the Manifesto in unduly inflammatory language, which, he felt, would only serve to alienate white liberal supporters. In the end, however, he lent his prestigious name to its sponsorship; but Roy Wilkins of the NAACP and Whitney Young of the Urban League refused to do so, giving as their reason the probable adverse effect of a blanket indictment of American institutions on the chances of passage of a pending civil rights bill then before the US Congress.

As the subsequent march progressed, so too did the split between moderates and radicals, with Dr Luther King struggling, as he continued to do until his voice was silenced in 1968 by an assassin's bullet, to retain the centre. In his *Where Do We Go From Here?*, King provided some poignant recollections of the manner in which the militants gained strength during the Meredith March.[1] He wrote, for example, of how he slowly came to realise that, as the marchers periodically paused to sing the famous civil rights song, 'We Shall Overcome', younger blacks were remaining silent when they came to the stanza which speaks of 'black and

[1] Martin Luther King, Jr, *Where Do We Go From Here: Chaos or Community?* (New York, 1967), Chapter 2.

white together'. One marcher told King that, if the militants had their way, the slogan 'We Shall Overcome' was going to be replaced by 'We Shall Overrun'. When, on the evening of June 17, the marching column reached Greenwood, Mississippi, a youthful orator named Stokely Carmichael, who had already made a name for himself among younger adherents of the movement, roused a mass meeting gathered in a city park, by saying:

'The only way we gonna stop them white men from whuppin' us is to take over. We been saying freedom for six years and we ain't got nothin'. What we gonna start saying now is *black power*.'[2]

At this pronouncement, Carmichael's friend and fellow member of SNCC, Willy Ricks, leaped to the platform and shouted to the crowd 'What do you want?', and, tired but exhilarated by Carmichael's rhetoric, they shouted back 'Black Power', and kept repeating it until their chant had reached fever pitch. Thus, while a national television audience looked on alarmed, there was launched a new, disturbing slogan in the militant doctrinal style.

Black power, of course, was not born during the Meredith March. Its roots lay deeply embedded in the complex historical pattern of racial tensions which Tocqueville, Acton, Bryce and others writing in the nineteenth century pointed to as a likely source of continued malaise in the American body politic.[3] Indeed, the stubborn persistence of white racialist bullying has been the mainstay of countless indictments of America by foreign commentators as well as by Americans, both black and white, and it cannot therefore by this late date have been a very original thought for oppressed blacks to yearn for a sort of millenarian turn of the racial tables. Nat Turner, after all, is as much a part of the

[2] Cited in B. Chambers (ed.), *Chronicles of Negro Protest* (New York, 1968), p. 270.

[3] For an historical perspective, see Floyd Barber (ed.), *The Black Power Revolt* (Boston, 1968), Section I.

black American experience as is Uncle Tom and Marcus Garvey no less so than Booker T. Washington.

The special poignancy of the militant Carmichael's cry of 'Black Power', however, lay in its having been sounded at the close of a decade during which, it could be fairly claimed, the dogged efforts of a loose, inter-racial coalition of liberal reformers had resulted in greater headway being made towards improved race relations than during any comparable period in American history. By the time of the victorious March on Washington in August, 1963, for example, the eloquent pleading of the world's leading orator and advocate of non-violence and Christian love seemed to have carried the day for gradualism. Martin Luther King's magnificent 'I Have a Dream' speech, delivered from the steps of the Lincoln Memorial to a crowd of a quarter million black and white supporters, was, politically speaking, nothing less than an oratorical essay on the practicality of working steadily for change from within the rules of the established order. 'I have a dream,' King said in the course of his remarks,

> 'that one day on the red hills of Georgia the sons of former slaves and the sons of former slave-holders will be able to sit down together at the table of brotherhood.'

His words were a eulogy to the effectiveness of the strategy of non-violence and integration, which, in the years following *Brown v. Board of Education* (1954), had yielded such impressive results as the successful Montgomery bus boycotts, the civil rights sit-ins, the freedom rides and, still in the future, the major civil rights legislation of 1964 and 1965.

Yet despite such substantial evidence of improvement, a recent comprehensive survey of the civil rights movement during the 1960s[4] shows that something had gone seriously wrong in the brief span of time separating the Washington march of 1963 and the Meredith shooting in 1966. Retrospectively, we know too well that while the voice of liberal

[4] Benjamin Muse, *The American Negro Revolution* (Bloomington, Indiana, 1968).

improvement held the field, other forces were at work in the dark ghettoes of America's great cities, forces that exploded upon the public consciousness when the worst peacetime rioting in American history occurred in the Watts section of Los Angeles during August, 1965, barely a week after the signing into law of the civil rights act of that year. The Watts incident, long before the explicit demand for 'Black Power' was sounded during the Meredith March, and long before any full public awareness of its significance, served notice that a new chapter was opening in the continuing American racial tragedy. In subsequent years, Newark, Detroit, Chicago, New Haven, Cleveland – even the nation's capital itself – became the leading names in a drama of violence on so large a scale that it engulfed virtually every major metropolitan area in America. By the middle of the decade, the old slogans of 'Freedom Now' and 'We Shall Overcome' seemed to lack the appeal, for many blacks and a dwindling band of their militant white supporters, of 'Black Power'. Since then, we have witnessed the translation of the prevailing dissatisfaction into the doctrinal rhetoric of 'Burn, Baby, Burn', 'Violence Is As American As Cherry Pie' and 'Oink To The Pigs'.

Undoubtedly, something *had* gone wrong. But what lay behind the appeal of the new wave of militancy is a question of many dimensions. In a sense, the 'civil rights' strategy of the moderates was rendered obsolete by its own successes. Once the formal legal and political barriers to participation were successfully challenged in the courts, the focus in the movement began to shift to the broader and more delicate problem of how guarantees of equal socio-economic opportunities might be achieved. No longer, in this new perspective, was the stereotyped setting of the rural South, where legal restrictions brazenly imposed on blacks under the 'separate but equal' doctrine had for years rendered Southern politics, in the national view, synonymous with racialism, the primary concern of the Negro reformer. The *de facto* racial injustices of sprawling, urban America, the systematic separation of life in the decaying central city Negro neighbourhoods from the comfortable white middle-class suburbs were now seen by radical blacks as the real *bête blanche*. This was a problem that was truly national in scope, and regional caricatures would simply no longer do as the whipping-boys for America's professed ideological egalitarianism.

Many Southern Negroes had learned that bitter truth at first hand when, as believers in the American Economic Dream, they streamed North in record numbers after World War II and Korea in search of a better life, only to be met by the flight of whites out of city centres and into new suburban sanctuaries. Forced by the harsh economics of urban racial exclusion into the already overburdened slums, the plight of the ghetto blacks steadily worsened at the same time that white Americans were enjoying an era of unprecedented material well-being. So too, of course, were some Negroes, who were getting ahead as never before in the armed services, in government, the universities and the professions; but 'some' was far from 'many', and farther still from 'most'.

In the circumstances, the anomalies of the established socio-economic order seemed proof enough to many young Negroes of the hollowness of the 'civil rights' victories of the early 1960s. Speeches on the virtues of gradualism no longer fell on receptive ears, when evidence such as that submitted by the Presidential Commission on Violence soberly suggested the real possibility of armed racial camps in urban America in the foreseeable future, where whites, during daytime forays into the predominantly Negro core cities, would be protected by private white armies against guerrilla attacks by frustrated black gangs, until safely returned to their suburban homes. Resentment, despondency and rage have been the reactions of many Negroes, and a Hobbesian 'state of nature' has seemed at times to dominate the racial scene. The Negro playwright, LeRoi Jones, speaks to an attentive audience when he suggests that nowadays 'Afro-Americans certainly have enough to hate', and adds:

'I am in favor of no kind of Negro protest that does not distress the kind of ethical sterility . . . liberalism represents. . . . There is a growing number of Negroes who are not willing to be bashed over the head or have their homes bombed to prove that Mr Gandhi was right.'[5]

The new generation of urban Negro leaders – typically self-educated 'para-intellectuals' of the hard-knocks school, products of the ghetto street corner, who have to a great extent replaced the older, university-educated 'black bourgeois' leadership as the heroes of the young[6] – reflect this new mood of black Americans in their cynicism towards liberal gradualism and their disdain for the pluralistic operating assumptions of the American political system.

While a number of organisations in the big American cities speak for Negro militancy, two have become especially well known: the Student Non-violent Co-ordinating Committee ('SNCC' or 'Snick') and the Black Panther Party. Stokely Carmichael, who was formerly Chairman of SNCC, and Eldridge Cleaver, the exiled Panther 'Minister of Information', have been widely regarded as the leading theorists of these groups, and of the 'Black Power' movement in general. In their writings and speeches we find interwoven the two main themes of 'Black Power': the psychologically-based notion of Negro racial pride and cultural nationalism, and the political ideology of revolutionary and radical-utopian change currently in vogue among the 'New Left'.

II

In 1960 a group of Negro students from North Carolina Agricultural and Technical College successfully 'sat in' for the first time at the previously 'whites only' luncheon counter of the Woolworth's department store in Greensboro, North Carolina. Pleased with the outcome of this pilot project, Dr Luther King's Southern Christian Leadership

[5] LeRoi Jones, *Home: Social Essays* (London, 1968), pp. 65–6.
[6] On this point, see the special issue of *Dissent* devoted to 'Black Power', July–August, 1969.

Conference agreed to advance them $800 to launch a more ambitious campaign. In this way, SNCC was born. It lost little time in showing how it differed from its parent organisation. From the beginning SNCC was a more militant outfit than the old civil rights groups and sought direct action confrontations as one of its press releases put it 'not as a means to integration, but as an effort to arouse black people to push for political power'. Its youthful leaders gave top priority to mobilising the latent power bloc of Negro voters emerging in the 1960s from the long winter of disenfranchisement; and it went about that task with an abrasiveness not usual in the style of the more established leadership.

SNCC first came to national prominence through the exploits of its bold young black and liberal white supporters in registering voters in Mississippi and Alabama, and through its sponsorship of the Mississippi Freedom Democratic Party, an unofficial half-black, half-white slate of nominees which unsuccessfully challenged the seating of the regular Mississippi delegation before the Credentials Committee of the National Democratic Party convention at Atlantic City in 1964.

Doctrinally, SNCC became increasingly extreme. In 1966, when Stokely Carmichael emerged as its Chairman, SNCC startled liberals by expelling and severing all connections with its liberal white supporters. The SNCC claimed that the older Negro organisations, like the NAACP, had lost credibility with young blacks because they had been subverted by the 'white liberal establishment'. Prestigious leaders, like the NAACP's Roy Wilkins, were styled as 'white men born with black skins'; psychologically, SNCC felt, whites, no matter how well-intentioned, were instinctively compelled to infiltrate and moderate black political organisations so as to avert the 'potential slave revolts' they feared in undiluted black mobilisation. In a so-called SNCC 'position paper' of 1966, it was argued that 'If we are to proceed towards true liberation, we must cut ourselves off from white people. We must form our own institutions, credit unions, co-ops, political parties, write our own histories.'[7] The SNCC message was not, moreover, solely one of cultural nationalism and Negro self-respect. It emphasised as well the revolutionary preparedness deemed necessary to achieve that goal in a hostile political culture.

SNCC has always been impatient with the 'turn the other cheek' tone of the more moderate rights groups. Frustrated by the intransigence of white race-haters, its youthful membership tended to emphasise physical preparedness and 'self-defence' as a more useful form of insurance against racial bullying than reliance on a belief in Christian brotherhood. Thus, in 1967, the controversial SNCC leader, H. Rapp Brown, suggested that 'The white man won't get off our backs, so we're going to knock him off. . . . If it comes to the point that black people must have guns, we will have means and ways to obtain those guns.' During 1969, SNCC's acceptance of Brown's argument, which discredited the organisation in the eyes of most moderate Negroes, was reflected in the announcement that it had officially dropped the word 'Non-violent' from its name.

The dual imagery of racial pride and revolution converges in the utterances of SNCC's most celebrated spokesman, Stokely Carmichael. By any measure, Carmichael must be accounted one of the most remarkable Negro leaders to emerge in the 1960s. His meteoric rise to political fame first brought the message of 'Black Power' to a wide audience. Tall and athletic, endowed with considerable physical presence and handsome features, Carmichael's chief political asset has been a rare facility of oratorical showmanship, which, as someone has suggested, is at times like 'the anti-white fulminations of Malcolm X . . . at times a harangue of Spartacus to the Roman gladiators, at times the senseless bawling of an angry child'.[8]

Carmichael was born in Trinidad and lived there until he

---

[7] Cited in T. Wagstaff (ed.), *Black Power: The Radical Response to White America* (New York, 1969), p. 115.
[8] B. Muse (*op. cit.*), p. 235.

was eleven, when his parents moved to New York. His father, a hard-working, upwardly mobile West Indian carpenter, did not like living among the 'unambitious' American Negroes of Harlem, where the family first settled, so he bought a house in a tough Italian neighbourhood of the East Bronx, which was 'balanced by a Jewish neighbourhood and an Irish neighbourhood'. As the only black-skinned family in their neighbourhood, the Carmichaels were a cut above the poverty-ridden Negroes of the New York ghettoes. Stokely was clearly also well above the intellectual norm; in 1956 he was chosen to attend the Bronx High School of Science, one of America's leading secondary schools. There were only fifty Negroes among two thousand students.

It was, in a sense, Carmichael's isolation in a white world that first led him to question the status accorded to the Negro in America. In Trinidad, the police, teachers, ministers, civil servants and merchants had as often as not been black-skinned; in America, Carmichael soon discovered, immediate authority was invariably wielded by whites. At Bronx High School his suspicions were fired by his association with 'a lot of people on the Left, young socialists', and he later recalled that he had 'always been oriented to the Left, from an economic point of view – not an economic determinist but certainly with a great proclivity for that sort of thing'.[9]

During his high school years Carmichael experienced a serious crisis of racial identity. While he was pressed by his parents to adopt the white middle-class standards to which they aspired, he had continued, after moving to the Bronx, to see his Negro friends in Harlem. Now he decided that it would be best for him to cut himself off from them altogether and to associate exclusively with his white school friends. But, hard as he tried to reject his black skin, Carmichael found that the white society in which he moved would not let him. He was a 'captive Negro', even among his well-meaning

[9] The discussion of this section draws on the interview with Carmichael reproduced in Robert Penn Warren, *Who Speaks for The Negro?* (New York, 1965), pp. 390–404.

peers. Some of his school acquaintances, intent on demonstrating their broad-mindedness, matched Carmichael's earnest attempts to submerge himself in 'their' culture with renewed efforts at 'going Fantee', however painful the unintended caricatures that resulted; and, as a bright and articulate student, Carmichael was constantly called on, in matters of student politics, to represent the 'Negro' point of view. At the very time he was trying to forget his race and find acceptance solely on grounds of his human qualities, then, Stokely felt he was being sought out and befriended by whites *because* he was a Negro.

He remembered, years later, an incident during this period which seemed to him to epitomise the cultural dilemma in which he found himself at Bronx High School: leaving a party at the fashionable Park Avenue penthouse of a white school friend's mother, he overheard his liberal-minded hostess say to one of her female guests, 'Oh yes, we let Jimmy hang around with Negroes.'

The eventual outcome of Carmichael's 'identity crisis' was that he gave up the attempt to integrate himself into white ways. He had learned, in the painful experience of growing up black, the paradox of 'making it' as a Negro in America. Success was purchased at the cost of accepting the very 'white' standards that were responsible for the Negro's self-consciousness about his supposed inferiority. To accept assimilation into the white *ethos*, to defer to white stereotypes of the 'Negro-American' (the phrase itself suggests the anomaly), was to contribute to the perpetuation of the state of affairs that produced in the Negro his characteristically mutilated self-esteem. The black American, he came to think, must affirm his cultural and racial *differences* from whites in order to gain psychological and spiritual release from his persistent self-abnegation.

Eventually Carmichael sought outlets for his growing convictions in active political participation. While still in high school in 1960 he took part in his first civil rights sit-in in Virginia, and his decision, upon graduation, to continue his studies at the predominantly Negro Howard University in

Washington, D.C. (where he majored in philosophy), when he had the opportunity of attending more celebrated institutions elsewhere, was prompted by his involvement in the politics of the civil rights movement. What attracted Carmichael to join the young blacks who took part in the rights sit-ins was not so much the doctrine of non-violence and Christian love upon which their campaigns were based, but rather the practical results in terms of self-discipline and 'inner power' that seemed to flow from their faith in the moral superiority of their cause. Beatings and jail sentences, as Martin Luther King had himself long contended, could not diminish the new-found sense of racial pride shared by adherents of the movement.

Carmichael was impressed by the short-term results of the moderates' campaign, but he rejected the ideological gradualism of Dr King's doctrine of love as 'nonsense' and 'euphemistic', since he believed that 'men always cover up their actions with moral issues', and would continue to resist effective change while theoretically accepting the integrationist ethic. The sit-ins gave Carmichael a more forceful idea than distant dreams of improvement in the future; they showed him glimpses of a latent racial power that, if it could be harnessed to a more powerful rhetoric and programme, might produce speedier political results. It is to precisely this point that Carmichael's formulation of the doctrine of 'Black Power' speaks.

Carmichael's fullest statement of his political ideas is contained in his *Black Power: The Politics of Liberation in America* (1967), written in conjunction with Charles Hamilton of Roosevelt University in Chicago. The book, according to the authors, 'presents a political framework and ideology which represents the last reasonable opportunity for this society to work out its racial problems short of prolonged destructive guerrilla warfare'. In it, a crucial distinction is drawn between the 'individual racism' of the negrophobe and the more subtle 'institutionalised racism' which, it is argued, permeates American society and poses the real obstacle to effective reform.

Institutionalised racism is depicted, in a discussion that borrows heavily from Frantz Fanon's *The Wretched of the Earth*, as merely another term for colonialism, and includes the various dimensions of control over blacks exercised by the 'white power structure'. The authors try to formulate an ideological overview that will tie the black American experience to the politics of liberation in the 'Third World'. Thus, politically, the celebrated pluralism of the American institutional fabric, it is asserted, becomes 'as monolithic as Europe's colonial offices have been to African and Asian colonies' whenever race enters the picture. Economically, white-inspired private and public 'uplift services' are accused of imposing a dehumanising paternalism on blacks, and so producing a pattern of race relations analogous to the relationship of do-gooding white missionaries to the indigenous populations of the colonial world. Socially, it is claimed, white racism has imposed on the black American a reign of 'cultural terror' under which he has been systematically relegated to an inferior status in the society.

While Carmichael nowhere offers a constructive programme of action, certain themes recur in *Black Power* in the various case-study chapters on such topics as the relative success of the SNCC Lowndes County, Alabama, voting drive, the failure of the Mississippi Freedom Democratic Party to gain national recognition, the hesitancy of the moderate black leadership of predominantly-Negro Tuskegee, Alabama, to seize power from the white minority, and the implications of the big city ghetto riots for the future direction of Negro politics in America, all of which enable us to piece together a programme for transforming the American system. In the first place, Carmichael reiterates his view that 'Afro-Americans' will never regain their autonomy unless they reject the white man's stereotypes of their race, and take pride in their African heritage. Culturally, the goal of blacks must be to reject assimilation into middle-class America, and positively to affirm their preference for their blackness. Moreover, *Black Power* argues that the psychological emancipation of black Americans will be to a large extent dependent on the adoption of new political strategies with which to combat more effectively the realities of a 'racist society'.

Carmichael's political programme is, in fact, based on the premise that 'Before a group can enter the open society, it must first close ranks'; priority must be given to the political goals of 'black self-determination', 'black self-identity' and 'black racial solidarity'. This means abandoning the slogans of the early civil rights movement for 'The language of yesterday is indeed irrelevant: progress, non-violence, integration, fear of 'white backlash', coalition....'

Liberals are Carmichael's particular bugbear, a point amply brought out, so far as political liberalism is concerned, in his *Black Power* chapter on 'The Myths of Coalition'. The theme is equally central in his other writings and speeches. Liberal pluralists, Carmichael believes, have successfully foisted on American historiography the 'melting pot' myth, whereby it is assumed that the assimilation of America's ethnic groups to the 'Anglo-conforming' standards of the general society has followed the classic pattern of coalition-building and integrationist politics. Carmichael suggests that what really happened was that 'by building Irish Power, Italian Power, Polish Power, or Jewish Power ... these groups got themselves together and operated from positions of strength'. He goes on to derive a lesson for blacks: first the interests of excluded ethnic minorities have not coincided with those of other reform groups, and then the picture is further complicated, where Negroes are concerned, by the persistence of institutionalised racism. Whites, he argues, do more harm than good when they attempt to join forces with black rights groups, for they have the effect of diluting the racial strength of such groups. Instead of infiltrating Negro political organisations, Carmichael suggests elsewhere, liberal whites should 'go into their own communities, which is where the racism exists'. He goes on to say:

'They want to run from Berkeley to tell us what to do in Mississippi; let them look instead at Berkeley. They admonish blacks to be non-violent; let them preach non-violence in the white community. They come to teach us

Negro history; let them go to the suburbs and open up freedom schools for whites. Let them work to stop America's racist foreign policy; let them press their government to cease supporting the economy of South Africa.'[10]

Equally unequivocally, Carmichael rejects the arguments of economic liberalism, and asserts that for racism to die 'a totally different America must be born'. He writes:

'Yes, I would like to see the government take over US Steel, General Motors, all the big corporations. I'd like to see more than one hundred people control over 60 per cent of the industry. I'd like to see all these plantations divided up until everybody who was on the plantation had his plot of land, because, like Mrs Hamer said: "Who the hell's land is it anyway?"'[11]

If a group politics of mutually compatible interests is ever to appear feasible to Afro Americans, he feels, the natural allies of blacks will be poor whites rather than middle-class liberals. 'The society we seek to build among black people', he writes elsewhere, 'is not a capitalist one. It is a society in which the spirit of community and humanistic love prevail.'

Carmichael does not appear to think this latter goal at all inconsistent with his critique of another tenet of liberalism, which we might term its moralism. According to Carmichael, it is naïve to think that political alliances are or can be sustained on a 'moral, friendly, sentimental basis; by appeals to conscience'. Mutual respect will only be forthcoming when there is some element of threat on both sides ('Political Power Grows Out of the Barrel of a Gun', as one of the modish slogans of contemporary radicalism has it). This is an argument relied on by Carmichael and SNCC to qualify the usual liberal injunctions against violence. For the black to subscribe categorically to the principle of non-violence in a racist society would be suicide; black people must be pre-

[10] B. Chambers (*op. cit.*), p. 277.
[11] Cited in Howard Zinn, *SNCC: The New Abolitionists* (Boston, 1965), p. 274.

pared to 'fight back'. At one level, the attack on economic liberalism and the rejection of the principle of non-violence coincide. For example, in the course of a speech delivered at the Congress on the Dialectics of Liberation, held in London during July, 1967, Carmichael asserted:

'I'm a political activist and I don't deal with the individual. I think it's a cop-out when people talk about the individual. What we're talking about around the US today, and I believe around the Third World, is the system of international white supremacy coupled with international capitalism. And we're out to smash that system. And people who see themselves as part of that system are going to get smashed with it – or we're going to get smashed.'[12]

The philosophy of non-violence and integration, according to Carmichael, no longer has credibility among the 'black proletariat', and after 1967, his enunciation of that theme became increasingly more emphatic. Non-violence, he submitted,

'could never attract and hold the young bloods who clearly understood the savagery of white America, and who were ready to meet it with armed resistance ... The Black Power movement has been the catalyst for the bringing together of these young bloods – the real revolutionary proletariat, ready to fight by any means necessary for the liberation of our people.'[13]

The cost of the attempt by black Americans to co-exist peacefully with whites has been 'the physical and psychological murder of our peoples'. In a speech at Oakland, California, in February, 1968, Carmichael said that the world was 'clearly heading for a colour clash' and he pleaded that black people must arm themselves and prepare to become 'the executioners of our executioners'.

[12] Reprinted in David Cooper (ed.), *The Dialectics of Liberation* (Harmondsworth, 1968), p. 150.
[13] *Ibid*, p. 162.

III

Carmichael's Oakland speech was the occasion for his first public appearance since returning to America from a widely publicised tour of the 'revolutionary countries of the Third World', during which he had assailed 'American racist imperialism' with increasing vituperation. His presence at the California rally coincided with his appointment as 'Honorary Prime Minister' of the Black Panther Party, and the merger of SNCC with the Panthers.

In the course of his talk Carmichael denounced the co-alition the BPP had recently formed with the white radical Peace and Freedom Party and called instead for a Black United Front that would bring together all the forces of the black community in a political machine capable of battering down, with force if necessary, the walls of white racism in America. Carmichael had, without any doubt, become more extreme in his pronouncements since the publication of *Black Power* in 1967.

On August 23, 1968, the *New York Times* reported that SNCC had by that date terminated its relationship with Carmichael, amidst reports that he had 'equated black power with black violence'. Soon equally at odds with his new-found West Coast brethren, Carmichael resigned from the Panthers less than a year later, charging, in a letter made public on July 3, 1969, that 'the party has become dogmatic in its ideology'. All those who disagreed with the party line, he said, 'are lumped into the same category and labelled cultural nationalists, pork chop nationalists, reactionary pigs'. Eschewing all alliances between whites and blacks, Carmichael announced that he was leaving America for good to take up residence at Conakry, Guinea, where he would work as a 'Pan Africanist' for the liberation of Africa. The letter of resignation brought forth a searing rebuttal from Eldridge Cleaver who, speaking for the Panthers in the September, 1969, issue of *Ramparts* magazine, suggested that Carmichael's habit 'of looking at the world through black-coloured glasses' and his 'paranoia about white control' effectively barred his understanding of 'the business of building the type of revolutionary machinery that we need in the United States'.

The parting of the ways between the extreme cultural nationalists who followed Carmichael, and the Black Panthers, has, as Cleaver's letter suggests, revolved around the Panther's emphasis upon 'revolutionary nationalism' rather than 'cultural nationalism'. The difference has split the ranks of the black militants into two distinct camps. As the jailed Panther leader, Huey P. Newton, wrote in the August, 1969, issue of *Ebony*, so far from 'retreating to some ancient African behavior and culture', the Black Panther

> 'sees that there is no hope for cultural or individual expression, or even hope that his people can exist as a unique entity in a complex whole, as long as the bureaucratic capitalist is in control. The Black Panthers are revolutionary nationalists. We do not believe that it is necessary to go back to the culture of eleventh century Africa. In reality, we must deal with the dynamic present in order to forge a progressive future.'[14]

Yet the shifting of priorities in the Panther wing of the Black Power movement has done little to allay the fears of moderate blacks who, at least as is suggested by such evidence as the NAACP's publication *The Crisis*, for November, 1968, have felt compelled to speak out 'loud and clear' against black extremists of whatever ideological bent 'who are shrilly and insistently espousing *apartheid*: racism, including anti-Semitism, intimidation, and violence'.[15] The Panthers have felt themselves misrepresented by such characterisations, insisting that, as Mary Leary wrote in the *New Republic* for November 30, 1968, they are 'unique in being the one cohesive black militant organisation deliberately reaching out to link whites with their cause'. The whites in this case are not, as with SNCC, poor whites; the Panthers

---

[14] Huey P. Newton, 'The Black Panthers', *Ebony*, August, 1969, p. 110.

[15] *Newsday*, December 22, 1968.

claim the support for their cause of the militant white New Leftists of America's universities – the 'Honkies for Huey'.

Like other militant black organisations – the Sons of Watts, US, the Angry Young Black Men, the United Brothers, the Malcolm X Society, the New Breed – the Panther leadership raises questions in the minds of moderates about the means they condone for effecting the changes they wish to see. To the general public, the youthful Panthers, in their black berets and leather jackets, shotguns at their sides and perhaps bullet-belts over the shoulder, have become synonymous with that irrational exhortation to violence which they regard as the central theme in the rhetoric of the New Left. The motto of the Panthers, a quotation from Mao Tse-tung's *Little Red Book*, does not help to clarify matters:

'We are advocates of the abolition of war; we do not want war; but war can only be abolished through war; and in order to get rid of the gun it is necessary to pick up the gun.'[16]

In an interview Huey Newton once asserted that 'I'm not anti-white. I don't hate a person because of the colour of his skin. I hate the oppression that we're subjected to daily by racist pigs and other racists who attack and murder and brutalise us.'[17] The very identification of hate as the motivation for Panther political activity, however, disturbs those who see too close an association of this feature of Panther rhetoric with the corollary argument of 'self-defence': 'The Panther never attacks first,' says Bobby Seale, a co-founder of the organisation, 'but once he is attacked he will respond viciously and wipe out the aggressor thoroughly, wholly, absolutely and completely.'[18]

The sad fact is that more than mere rhetoric has been in-

[16] Eldridge Cleaver, *Post-Prison Writings and Speeches* (New York, 1969), p. 37.
[17] Quoted in Bobby Seale and Eldridge Cleaver, 'Selections from the Biography of Huey P. Newton' (Part II), *Ramparts*, November 17, 1968, p. 56.
[18] Quoted in Mary Leary, 'The Uproar Over Cleaver', *New Republic*, November 30, 1968, p. 21.

volved. On a scale unmatched elsewhere in the politics of the New Left, violence *has* been a part of the revolutionary black nationalist movement. At least 19 Panthers (six at the hands of other black militants) and four policemen have died in shootings, and scores more on both sides have been injured. The pattern of violence has been too complex to identify a single source of the incitement: some of the incidents have been traced to police jumpiness, others to Panther harassment of police, and still others to internal Panther vendettas against 'counter-revolutionary' members. The Panthers urge that they are the victims of a police campaign to exterminate them, claiming moreover that the press and television have distorted their politics and ignored their positive role, like that of the Black Muslims, in sponsoring free breakfast programmes and other community welfare 'self-help' services in the ghettoes. While the Panthers believe they have accomplished much good for black Americans, it is undeniable that, caught in the web of their revolutionary rhetoric, they have also produced many roadblocks to racial understanding. There is the case of the colouring books for distribution among the Negro children of the San Francisco area (which the party leadership claimed were unauthorised by national headquarters), which depicted blacks shooting white policemen with pig-like features while Negro children looked on, with the caption 'Black Brothers Protect Black Children',[19] and there were Black Panther Christmas cards with this exchange between the Panther parent and wide-eyed child on the cover:

Panther: 'Son, what do you want for Christmas?'
Child: 'A machine-gun, shotgun, a box of hand grenades, a box of dynamite and a box of matches.'

The Black Panther Party was founded in 1966 by Huey P. Newton and Bobby Seale (now both in prison) who became friends in the early '60s after meeting at a street rally as students in Oakland, California. Newton, the Party's

[19] 'The Black Panthers', *Wall Street Journal*, August 29, 1969, pp. 1, 12.

'Minister of Defence', has been its acknowledged leader since then, even though he has been in prison since 1968, convicted of the voluntary manslaughter of an Oakland policeman. Seale's admiration for Newton, he has said, amounts to 'a sort of worship', and Eldridge Cleaver has added that his own feelings towards Newton involve 'the same willingness to place my life in his hands, the same confidence that Huey will do the right thing at any given moment, that his instincts are sound, and that there is nothing to do but follow Huey and back him up.'[20] There can be no doubt as to Newton's reckless brand of personal courage: armed with a loaded M-1 rifle and a law book, he would 'confront' and stare down police officers before black street corner crowds, verbally lacing them while urging his audience to 'stand up for their rights against the pigs'.

When the co-founders of the Panthers met, Newton was active in spreading interest in Malcolm X's Afro-American Association on the West Coast. He later became disillusioned with that organisation because it sought reform within the capitalist system, while Newton, who rejected the 'black capitalism' argument then in vogue, became convinced that socialism was needed to overcome the avarice of both the white and black *bourgeoisie* which, he believed, together kept black urban America in bondage.

Seale first introduced Newton to Fanon's *The Wretched of the Earth* and Newton eagerly seized upon it, as well as the works of Mao, Guevara and Malcolm X. Shortly afterwards, the two founded the Soul Students Advisory Council as an instrument to 'serve the black community in a revolutionary fashion'; it was out of the SSAC, and the Community Alert Patrol formed after the Watts riots that the Black Panther Party grew. In his *Biography of Huey P. Newton*, Bobby Seale recounts how the original group of Panthers in the Bay area forged a concrete bond uniting their Marxist-Maoist ideology with their Fanonist psychology, right under the nose of the

[20] Bobby Seale and Eldridge Cleaver, 'Selections from the Biography of Huey P. Newton' (Part I), *Ramparts*, October 26, 1968, p. 24.

capitalist system: they bought up copies of Mao's *Red Book* for 30 cents apiece at the China Book Store in San Francisco, sold them to white student 'joiners' in front of Sather Gate at Berkeley for a dollar a copy, and used the profits to purchase shotguns.[21]

The Black Panthers first came to national prominence when they made a sensational armed appearance in the corridors of the California state legislature in May, 1967, protesting against a law banning the carrying of weapons in public which had been rushed through partly as a response to the Panther strategy of armed 'confrontation' of police in the San Francisco area. While small (a *Life* estimate of February 6, 1970, places total membership at around 1,200), the Party today claims to have local chapters in at least two dozen of America's major cities. Its popularity among blacks has thus been limited, but, as Cleaver has asserted, the Panthers attribute this to the fact that 'Black people are afraid to join a militant group. They're afraid the cops will shoot them. That's just why we made the cops our political target – to prove to the brothers that cops are just fat, gristle and blood.' The Party has recently experienced a certain upsurge in its popularity in the aftermath of the slaying of the Illinois Chairman, Fred Hampton, by a Special Forces section of the Chicago police department.

Organisationally, the Party displays many of the characteristic features of the classic cadre party. For information purposes, there is an official organ of party opinion, *The Black Panther* newspaper, some 100,000 copies of which are distributed weekly. There is an official ten-point Party Programme, drawn up in October, 1966, and presumably unintentionally imitative of a statement rendered in a similar format in the *Communist Manifesto*:

1. We want freedom. We want power to determine the destiny of our Black Community.
2. We want full employment for our people.

[21] *Ibid*, p. 30.

3. We want an end to the robbery by the CAPITALIST of our Black Community.

4. We want decent housing, fit for shelter of human beings.

5. We want education for our people that exposes the true nature of this decadent American society. We want education that teaches us our true history and our role in the present-day society.

6. We want all black men to be exempt from military service.

7. We want an immediate end to POLICE BRUTALITY and MURDER of black people.

8. We want freedom for all black men held in federal, state, county and city prisons and jails.

9. We want all black people when brought to trial to be tried in court by a jury of their peer group or people from their black communities, as defined by the Constitution of the United States.

10. We want land, bread, housing, education, clothing, justice and peace. And as our major political objective, a United Nations-supervised plebiscite to be held throughout the black colony, in which only black colonial subjects will be allowed to participate, for the purpose of determining the will of black people as to their national destiny.[22]

Furthermore, the Party has established a list of some 26 Party Rules, which BPP members must commit to heart; some of these rules define the relations of command between the National Headquarters Central Committee and local chapters and branches, some govern behaviour (for example, 'No party member can have narcotics or weed in his possession while doing party work'; 'No party member can be DRUNK while doing daily party work'; 'No party member will USE, POINT or FIRE a weapon of any kind unnecessarily or accidentally at anyone') and some are simple Maoist-like exhortations to improvement: 'Everyone in a leadership

[22] As reprinted in *The Black Panther* for January 24, 1970, p. 19.

position must read at least two hours per day to keep abreast of the changing political situation.' Newton himself drew up an organisational '10-10-10 programme' for encouraging party solidarity. According to the evidence of Mrs Jean Powell, former BPP national secretary, testifying before the Senate Permanent Investigations Sub-Committee during 1969:

> 'The 10-10-10 plan structure was to take a map of the city, cut the city into 10 sections, over each section there would be a section leader, take the 10 sections, cut them into 10 subsections, over each . . . a subsection leader, take the 10 subsections, cut them into 10 block sections and there was a block leader. In the event of police harassment of a black person, you could call from your block to your block leader who would get some type of defense to the person being harassed. . . . The bigger the problem, got, the higher you went into subsections and sections. Such as a mass thing, like a riot, all 10 sections would be dispatched.'[23]

Talking the language of 'self defence', the Black Panthers prepared for guerrilla warfare against the 'fascist pig' police should other avenues to their demands become closed.

The best-known Black Panther is Eldridge Cleaver, who came to national prominence as one of the most gifted of younger black writers with the publication of his best-selling *Soul on Ice* in 1968. In his own way Cleaver is perhaps an even more remarkable figure than Stokely Carmichael. If Carmichael is a black revolutionary whose intellectual journey carried him to the camp of Negro cultural nationalism, Cleaver might rather be depicted as a black cultural critic who has ended in the arms of the revolutionaries. His friend Robert Scheer, who saw Cleaver in Algiers in July, 1969, reported that 'he was now calling himself a "Marxist-Leninist" universalist'. But he was not always a radical dreamer of programmatic political change: in his early essays, Cleaver is preoccupied with the separable question of

[23] Quoted in *The Spivack Report*, IV (4), June 30, 1969.

identifying the Negro cultural style in the American social landscape. The change of pace came after he was released from Folsom Prison: it was then, in February, 1967, that he met the Black Panthers for the first time; it was, as he recalled, a case of 'literally love at first sight'.[24]

In some ways Cleaver reminds one of Jean Genet; in others, however, he seems to be a sort of Eric Hoffer-in-reverse of the radical black movement in America ('the apotheosis of the American nightmare', as he has latterly mockingly self-portrayed himself; 'loudmouthed nigger, ex-convict, rapist, advocate of violence, Presidential candidate'). There is, of course, no similarity whatever in the political views of Hoffer and Cleaver: what I have in mind is their shared sense of pride in their self-education.

Those sections of *Soul on Ice* dealing with Cleaver's prison years are, in this respect, a monument erected by the author to his persistence and discipline in mastering the craft of letters amidst the grim atmosphere of prison life. His pages abound with references to Rousseau, Paine and Voltaire, Richard Wright, Paul Goodman and Thomas Merton, Baldwin and Mailer, Hinduism, Zen Buddhism, Thomas Wolfe and Ashley Montagu. And yet there is another side to Cleaver which seems to urge a kind of primitivism, a break with the restraints of reason, of culture, of 'objectivity', that speaks to the emotions of black men whose psychological health, he believes, has been destroyed by the cultural regalia of white 'civilisation'.

In Cleaver's recent *Playboy* story, 'The Flashlight', Stacy Mims is a young Negro who loves life in the streets of his deteriorating Los Angeles neighbourhood and who experiences 'freedom' as a kind of psychological autonomy that is dependent on identifying with his own kind; Stacy felt

'he was losing it each time he set foot on the school grounds . . . the whole situation repelled him. He felt that

[24] Eldridge Cleaver, 'The Courage to Kill: Meeting the Panthers', *Post-Prison Writings and Speeches*, p. 23.

books and the knowledge in them were part of a world that was against him, a world to which he did not belong and which he did not want to enter, the world of which the hateful teachers were representatives and symbols. After school each day it took several blocks of walking before he was free of its field of force. Then he blossomed, felt himself. His pace quickened and became his own again.'[25]

The same theme is amply evident elsewhere in Cleaver's work, as, for example, in his *Soul on Ice* essay on '"The Christ" and His Teachings', where he narrates the pathetic story of the do-gooding prison teacher, Chris Lovdjieff. In fact, Cleaver never really succeeds in overcoming the tension between intellectual reasoning and irrationalism in his writings; at times, he seems to recommend the use of books as a panacea for the plight of black Americans, while at others he urges Negroes to 'get the gun', threatening that 'We shall have our manhood. We shall have it or the earth will be leveled by our attempts to gain it.'

Cleaver once described himself as 'extremist by nature',[26] a self-characterisation that helps to explain his way of writing. One critic has suggested that the force of Cleaver's literary style rests on 'an inspired and wild prose that tends to subvert rational judgment . . . one reads Cleaver not for argument or program but for the affective experience. In the end, rhetoric blurs thought.'[27] The same might be said for his life-style. Cleaver is reported to be a man who enjoys solitude, the result, presumably, of his long periods alone in prison. The same considerations may explain the urgent tone in which his political and social commentary is cast. Cleaver is a man with a lot of 'catching up' to do, a man to whom opposition poses inconveniences he is unwilling to tolerate. In a 'Note to My Friends' which appeared in

[25] Eldridge Cleaver, 'The Flashlight', *Playboy*, December, 1969, pp. 122-4.

[26] Eldridge Cleaver, *Soul on Ice* (New York, 1968), p. 16.

[27] Stanley Pacion, 'Eldridge Cleaver: Soul Still on Ice?', *Dissent*, July–August, 1969, p. 310.

Ramparts for September, 1969, Cleaver characteristically asserted that 'I dig life. And when I die, my death will be the price I paid to live. Right on! Power to the People. Oink to the pigs.'

Cleaver's background as a convict pervades his writings. The first part of *Soul on Ice*, indeed, is an extensive indictment of the prevailing notions of American penology. The prison system, he argues, is a racist institution for 'keeping down' blacks who are clever enough to challenge the system. Citing his own case, he suggests that, for the urban Negro, 'the cops [are] always somewhere, hovering, a vague presence, reeking the stink of a bad dream'. He recounts[28] how he was first sent to California's Juvenile Hall, for stealing a bicycle at the age of twelve; from there he 'graduated' steadily to Whittier Reform School, Preston School of Industries and the state penitentiary. Almost his entire adult life, until he fled the country rather than return to prison when his parole was revoked in 1968, has been spent in the demeaning and de-humanising jungle of prisons. Negro inmates, he suggests, do not regard themselves as criminals, but as 'prisoners of war, the victims of a vicious, dog-eat-dog social system that is so heinous as to cancel out their malfunctions.'

> 'Rather than owing and paying a debt to society, Negro prisoners feel that they are being abused, that their imprisonment is simply another form of the oppression which they have known all their lives. Negro inmates feel that they are being robbed, that it is "society" that owes them, that should be paying them, a debt.'[29]

Cleaver does not shrink from following the logic of his argument to its conclusion: defending the point in the BPP programme that calls for the release of all Negroes held in prisons, he suggests that they be handed over to the Black Panthers, who will put them to work, not in committing

---

[28] Eldridge Cleaver, 'The Black Moochie' (Part I), *Ramparts*, October, 1969, p. 22; 'An Address', *Ibid*, December 12, 1968, pp. 6–10.

[29] Eldridge Cleaver, *Soul on Ice*, p. 58.

minor robberies, but in planning the overthrow of the Bank of America, or Chase Manhattan Bank, or Brinks.[30]

Cleaver's view is that the psycho-sexual relationship of black and white Americans holds the key to racial mistrust. In *Soul on Ice*, he recalls how, as a denizen of the Negro 'criminal' subculture, he sought an outlet for his frustration in the senseless destruction of the artifacts of white American society. Indeed, he became a rapist of white women (having first, he explains, 'to refine my technique and *modus operandi* . . . started out by practising on black girls in the ghetto'), because rape was to him 'an insurrectionary act. It delighted me that I was defiling and trampling upon the white man's laws, upon his system of values, and that I was defiling his women . . . I felt I was getting revenge.'[31] During his last stay in prison, however, Cleaver resolved to 'straighten up and fly right'; sickened by his animalistic behaviour, he began to write, as he says, 'to save myself'.

Hence the analysis of the love-hate relationship of Negro and white Americans is given a primary focus in Cleaver's writings. Whether in the autobiographical recollections of his rebuffed schoolboy attentions to a white girl, Michele Ortago, or his sexual yearning for his white teacher, Mrs Brick 'of the fine ass and nice tits', or in the fictional 'Allegory of the Black Eunuchs', or in his extravagant profession of love for his white female lawyer, Beverly Axelrod (his *Soul on Ice* is dedicated to her), Cleaver is never far from the sexual theme (claiming in one place, in a bizarre twentieth-century version of the argument of Aristophanes's *Lysistrata*, that 'political power, revolutionary power, grows out of the lips of a pussy').[32]

In his extraordinary fantasy, 'The Primeval Mitosis', Cleaver differentiates four psycho-sexual types: whites comprise the 'Omnipotent Administrator' and the 'Ultra-

---

[30] Eldridge Cleaver, 'Farewell Address', *Post-Prison Writings and Speeches*, pp. 115–6.

[31] Eldridge Cleaver, *Soul on Ice*, p. 14.

[32] Eldridge Cleaver, 'Stanford Speech', *Post-Prison Writings and Speeches*, p. 143.

feminine Doll' categories, while blacks are relegated to the role of 'Supermasculine Menials' and 'Amazons'. The tragedy of America's having thus racially defined psycho-sexual types, he argues, is that all are equally frustrated: the omnipotent administrator, guardian of the priority of mind over body, is for that very reason unable fully to satisfy the longings of the ultrafeminine doll; the supermasculine menial, 'robbed of his brain' by white stereotypes, is held in low esteem by black women; and the amazon, in turn, views the omnipotent administrator as the male symbol of authority.

Had Cleaver stopped here he would merely have offered a restatement of the old racial stereotype of the Negro stud – he does, in fact, note rather condescendingly that the white American male often refers to his penis in such unheroic language as a 'prick', 'peter' or 'pecker'. But he seems to be saying more than that. The black male is the catalyst of racial emancipation, the symbol of virility, strength and power, the 'psychic bridegroom' of the white female, the saviour who can

> 'blaze through the wall of her ice, plumb her psychic depths, test the oil of her soul, melt the iceberg in her brain, touch her inner sanctum, detonate the bomb of her orgasm, and bring her sweet release.'[33]

Once blacks realise that they hold the key to free all alike from the society-wide prison of psycho-sexual repression, they will no longer be 'black eunuchs'; they will be awakened at last from the 400-year slumber of their past, at last able to call on their 'Black Beauty', their 'Sable Sister', their

> 'Queen-Mother-Daughter of Africa
> Sister of My Soul
> Black Bride of My Passion
> My Eternal Love'

to 'put on your crown, my Queen, and we will build a New City on these ruins'.[34]

[33] Eldridge Cleaver, *Soul on Ice*, pp. 185–6.
[34] Eldridge Cleaver, 'To All Black Women, From All Black Men', *Soul on Ice*, pp. 205–10. Also relevant here is his 'The Allegory of the Black Eunuchs' in the same collection.

The difficulty of this whole line of argument, of course, is that Cleaver assumes that the 'Supermasculine Menial' and the 'Amazon' are simply the 'least alienated from the biological chain'. Moreover, he asks us to accept as superior the claims of the body (black or any other colour) over those of the mind (white). This is a dubious proposition, made no more acceptable by his belief, expressed elsewhere, that 'In the world revolution now underway, the initiative rests with people of colour.'[35]

Politically, Cleaver's writings reflect the Black Panthers' ideological outlook. Reviewing Fanon's *The Wretched of the Earth* (which he identifies as 'the Bible' of the black liberation movement in America) during 1967, he noted that

'What this book does is legitimize the revolutionary impulse to violence. It teaches colonial subjects that it is perfectly normal for them to want to rise up and cut off the heads of the slavemasters, that it is a way to achieve their manhood, and that they must oppose the oppressor in order to experience themselves as men.'[36]

Opposition is at the core of Cleaver's politics; they are the politics of the rebel and iconoclast. In *The Black Moochie*, he describes himself as one who has 'something rigid in me, an inarticulate opposition, a dissent'.[37] And earlier, in his first book, he confesses that, in jail, '*because everybody seemed to find it necessary to attack* Karl Marx in their writings, I sought out his books, and although he kept me with a headache, I took him for my authority'.[38] His early readings in political philosophy led him to admire Bakunin, and Nechayev's *Catechism of the Revolutionist*, and in *Soul on Ice* he tells Beverly

[35] Eldridge Cleaver, 'The White Race and Its Heroes', *Soul on Ice*, p. 81.

[36] Eldridge Cleaver, 'Psychology: The Black Bible', *Post-Prison Writings and Speeches*, p. 20.

[37] Eldridge Cleaver, 'The Black Moochie' (Part I), *Ramparts*, October, 1969, p. 27.

[38] Eldridge Cleaver, *Soul on Ice*, p. 12 (emphasis added).

Axelrod, in the course of a letter written from prison, how he wishes he could 'grow a beard and don whatever threads the local nationalism might require and comrade with Che Guevara, and share his fate, blazing a new pathfinder's trail through the stymied upbeat brain of the New Left'.[39]

Since becoming a prominent member of the Panthers, Cleaver's wish has been amply fulfilled. Impatiently he has urged upon middle-class America (or 'Babylon', as he likes to call it) in numerous articles and essays that blacks have 'prayed in, we have crawled in, we have knelt in, everything', and that 'we're reaching the point today where words are becoming more and more irrelevant'.

Speaking at Stanford University in 1968, when he was the BPP/Peace and Freedom Party presidential candidate, Cleaver suggested that the basic problem in America today is 'political confusion', a confusion caused in large part by America's failure to address itself to the correction of the pervasive damages caused by racism. He warned that, unless America sat up and listened to its black militants, 'the niggers are going to come into the white suburbs and turn the white suburbs into shooting galleries'.[40]

IV

One is hard-pressed to avoid misrepresenting the proponents of 'Black Power'. In the absence of practical programmes of reform it is not always easy to see where their rhetoric is leading. While the co-author of the *Black Power* book, Charles Hamilton, has since its publication attempted, for example, in his article 'An Advocate of Black Power Defines It',[41] to illustrate that it is not an end in itself but an attempt at encouraging political discipline in the Negro community,

[39] *Ibid.*, p. 19.

[40] Eldridge Cleaver, 'Stanford Speech', *Post-Prison Writings and Speeches*, p. 127.

[41] *New York Times Magazine*, April 14, 1968, reprinted in T. Wagstaff (*op. cit.*), pp. 124–38. Hamilton is now at Columbia University.

many Negroes and white liberals nonetheless view with alarm the radicalism of such groups as SNCC and the Panthers, arguing that their theories amount to a kind of black or Third World racism. Certainly, there have been more critics of 'Black Power' than supporters.[42]

Dr King and his followers, as we have noticed, were, from the outset, disturbed by the slogan 'Black Power', fearing – and surely in retrospect their fears look justified – that its emotionalism would only serve to arouse white dread of black domination. Dr King himself rightly pointed to the dangers of dwelling on the rhetoric of 'self defence'. Fanon's thesis that violence is a psychologically healthy and tactically sound political outlet for the oppressed may, indeed, have an obvious appeal, as Carmichael has asserted, to the 'young bloods', but the point is to resist that appeal and channel it to constructive purposes.

No one in the moderate camp ever denied the right of individual self-defence; but to dwell on the rhetoric of violence, especially where crowds are concerned, is surely to produce more harm than good. It is no new idea in political thought that the line of demarcation between 'defensive violence' and 'aggressive violence' is a very thin one. Correspondingly, there is much evidence that, in the aftermath of the Negro resort to violence and destruction in the big American cities during the late '6os, it was the black community itself which suffered the worst damage.

It is now widely accepted that, as a psychological symbol for harnessing the pride and imagination of Negro Americans, the 'Black Power' slogan proffered a sense of urgency and occasion for younger blacks that the more moderate programmes and leadership did not. Yet the fact remains that the positive assertions of 'Black Power' have been outweighed by its negative features. However hard the Black

[42] For example, *Editorial Research Reports* (November 19, 1969), cites the result of a CBS Opinion Research study conducted in mid-1968, which reported that 1% of the Negroes interviewed would give active support to Ron Karenga, 2% to Rap Brown, 4% to Stokely Carmichael, and 49% to Ralph D. Abernathy, Dr King's successor.

Power people protest against their position being mis-represented, there is an important truth in the moderates' criticism that black power is a 'nihilistic philosophy' which represents 'a dashing of hope, a conviction of the inability of the Negro to win, and a belief in the infinitude of the ghetto'.[43]

This is a point of view which has for long been argued, for example, by Bayard Rustin, Executive Director of the A. Philip Randolph Institute and one of the most respected of moderate black leaders. Rustin rejects[44] the argument of radicals, who, stymied by the intransigence of the accepted American socio-political *mores*, have concluded that 'the only viable strategy is shock; above all, that the hypocrisy of white liberals must be exposed'. The cold fact remains that America's twenty million black people, some ten per cent of the total population, cannot win power alone; they need allies. Even with the growth of predominantly black urban centres, according to reputable authorities,[45] Negroes will have to join forces with some segment of the white community in order to achieve an effective political voice. In this perspective, Carmichael's premise that 'Before a group can enter the open society, it must first close ranks', may have a certain psychological meaning, but cannot be maintained as the basis of a useful political strategy. The notion that blacks will only be taken seriously if they succeed in frightening the white man will never sustain a serious political programme for the simple reason, as Rustin argues, that 'fear is more likely to bring hostility to the surface than respect'.

In his most recent book, *The Agony of the American Left*, Christopher Lasch has added his voice to those unimpeach-

[43] Martin Luther King, Jr, (*op. cit.*), p. 47.

[44] Bayard Rustin, 'From Protest to Politics: The Future of the Civil Rights Movement', *Commentary*, February, 1965, pp. 25–31; 'Coalition Politics', *ibid.*, September, 1966, pp. 35–40; 'The Myths of the Black Revolt', *Ebony*, August, 1969, pp. 96–104.

[45] See, for example, the *Congressional Quarterly's* 'Political Report' for September 12, 1969, pp. 1681–4.

ably committed to the goal of effecting racial equality yet critical of the claims of 'Black Power' as an ideological vehicle for achieving it. As a manifestation of the New Left, he suggests, Black Power

> 'shares with the white Left not only the language of romantic anarchism but several other features as well, none of them . . . conducive to its success – a pronounced distrust of people over thirty, a sense of powerlessness and despair, for which the revolutionary rhetoric serves to compensate, and a tendency to substitute rhetoric for political analysis and defiant gestures for political action.'[46]

Lasch suggests that 'Black Power' abounds in contradictions, its incoherence stemming from an inability of its leading theorists to make up their minds whether the black liberation movement is 'a class issue, a race issue, or a "national" (ethnic) issue'. There is a related criticism, perhaps best represented in Harold Cruse's devastating analysis of the theoretical foundations of 'Black Power', in his *The Crisis of the Negro Intellectual*, where it is argued that the reliance of rhetoricians of black militancy on a non-American theoretical apparatus, whether of the Marxian communist or Third World guerrilla warfare variety, amounts to 'a colossal fraud'.

Cruse's position is that Negro 'Black Power' advocates, whether styled 'Afro-Americans' or 'Black Americans', are merely play-acting with an imported ideological scenario, and forget that their 'brothers' *are* American Negroes, an integral part of the American political landscape.

In fact, he might extend the general criticism of the emptiness of the 'Black Power' ideological categories to embrace the theoretical distinction made between 'individual racism' and 'institutionalised racism' itself. Carmichael has defined individual racism as 'overt acts by individuals, with usually the immediate result of the death of victims, or the traumatic and violent destruction of property', whereas

[46] Christopher Lasch, *The Agony of the American Left* (New York, 1969), Chapter 4 (131).

institutionalised racism he regards as 'the overall operation of established and respected forces in the society [which thus do not] receive the condemnation that the first type receives'.[47]

Is the hazy notion of 'the overall operation' of 'established forces' any advance on the moderate's injunction to combat 'racial prejudice' wherever we find it? So far from helping to focus the problem, the idea of 'institutionalised racism' may actually contribute to an attitude of defeatism. Hannah Arendt has made a similar point:

'We all know . . . that it has become rather fashionable among white liberals to react to Negro grievances with the cry, "We are all guilty", and "black power" has proved only too happy to take advantage of this "confession" to instigate an irrational "black rage". When all are guilty, no one is; confessions of collective guilt are always the best possible safeguard against the discovery of the actual culprits.'[48]

There is an exchange between Alice and Humpty Dumpty in Lewis Carroll's *Alice in Wonderland* which rather nicely suggests the distance separating the moderates from the rhetoricians of 'Black Power'. It is a passage which Stokely Carmichael is fond of quoting, where Humpty Dumpty says 'When I use a word . . . it means what I choose it to mean. Neither more nor less.' The dialogue continues:

'The question is,' said Alice, 'whether you can make words mean so many different things.'
'The question is,' said Humpty Dumpty, 'who is to be master. That is all.'

Like Alice, the moderate questions whether the ideological terminology of 'Black Power' actually corresponds to the multifaceted reality of political life in America; like Humpty Dumpty, the black radical insists on framing his rhetoric in terms of the stipulative rigidities of 'Who is to be master'.

[47] Stokely Carmichael, 'Black Power', in D. Cooper (*op. cit.*), p. 151.
[48] Hannah Arendt, 'Reflections on Violence', *Journal of International Affairs*, XXIII (1), 1969, p. 25.

The Negro psychologist and author of *Dark Ghetto*, Kenneth B. Clark, once pointed out that 'heroics and dramatic words and gestures, oversimplified either/or thinking and devil-hunting, might provide a platform for temporary crowd-pleasing, ego satisfactions, or would-be "leaders", but they cannot solve the fundamental problem'.[49] To which line of argument Eldridge Cleaver truculently responds:

'... today ... you're either part of the solution or you're part of the problem. There is no middle ground ... All of you pigs who want to support the other side, just fuck you, pig, and I hope that some nigger catches you on a dark street and kills you ... All of those who are not going to choose that side, I love you. And I recognize your humanity and I hope you can recognize mine.'[50]

Psychologically, we might say, the friends of Cleaver and Carmichael share the sentiment expressed in the Beatle song-title that 'Happiness is a Warm Gun'; yet politically, they would have little sympathy with the lyrics of their 'Revolution', where they sing:

> 'We all want to change the world
> But when you talk about destruction
> Don't you know that you can count me out ...
> You say you got a real solution
> Well you know
> We'd all love to see the plan.'

It has been suggested that when the young Russian revolutionists of the 1870s convinced themselves that non-violent methods could never lead to satisfactory political results, they felt that a certain emotional threshold had been crossed. Extreme adherents of the 'Black Power' doctrine seem to find a similar emotional release. But in the end, we must ask ourselves whether 'Black Power' appeals to what is best

[49] Quoted in Robert Penn Warren (*op. cit.*), p. 317.

[50] Eldridge Cleaver, *Post-Prison Writings and Speeches*, p. xxxii.

For further expressions of Cleaver's views see Lee Lockwood, *Conversations with Eldridge Cleaver: Algiers* (New York, 1970) and Jerry Rubin, *Do It!* (New York, 1970).

in the American experience, or whether its force rests upon fear and the eulogising of the irrational. Does it offer a constructive answer to the complex problems of racial friction in a civilisation which, in some respects through its very commitment to ideological egalitarianism, has aroused social expectations that, temporarily at least, the political machinery seems incapable of effecting? Today in America as elsewhere there are doubtless many 'racists'; yet there are also many individuals of good will, and of all races, who patiently seek less self-conscious personal relations where race is concerned. Is one any better able to speak to the moral dimensions of the question, to the issues of social justice and human rights raised whenever practices of racial exclusion are involved, in terms of 'society', 'forces' or 'system', rather than 'persons' and 'individual development'?

I believe that 'Black Power' does not help to clarify these questions. They are, needless to say, big questions, the answers to which, one might plausibly contend, will be forthcoming only, if ever, when fears are eradicated, not aroused, where hatred is excised, rather than abetted, and where anxieties based on unsubstantiable behavioural myths are painstakingly rebutted and reduced at their source. In this respect, 'Black Power' has not been a useful and constructive doctrine. Indeed, in some ways it has been more than a merely confusing notion; it has endangered the very prospect of improvement. 'Black Power' blocks the road to the goal it claims to seek.

R. D. LAING

David Martin

R. D. LAING

David Martin

Ronald Laing must be accounted one of the main contributors to the theoretical and rhetorical armoury of the contemporary Left. By the contemporary left is meant that soft variant of the utopian urge which has jettisoned the Marx of *Capital* for the spiritual exploration of alienation, which acknowledges that capitalism 'delivers the goods to an ever increasing part of the population'[1] and therefore concentrates its attention on the salvation of the all-too-common man from what Marcuse calls 'one dimensionality'.

With the erosion of a proletarian communism, its confinement to institutional rigidity or its continuing commitment to Stalinoid deformations, one is left with a *salon* communism, whereby the Ortega y Gassets of the Left join forces with their conservative opposite numbers on the other side of high table in a lament for the regrettable tendencies of mass society. It is they who – to take an image of Laing's – are the lonely 'survivors' in a neo-capitalist civilisation which is condemned to swinish contentment; confined to the pleasures of consumption without appropriate refinement of palate. 'Consume more, live less' as one of the slogans has it. So pessimistic is this approach that hope is only thought possible by calling in a Third World to redress the balance of the two old ones.

This is the general and by now familiar picture presented by the 'soft left', and it is the aim of this essay to locate the place of R. D. Laing within its broad syndrome of attitudes. Unfortunately the term 'attitudes' is only too appropriate, since we are confronted here by a psychological set that positively avoids careful analysis and treats the notion of fact as a treacherous bourgeois invention. The old Left did at least propose an analysis and practised a policy in relation to

---

[1] *The Dialectics of Liberation*, ed. D. Cooper (Penguin, 1968), pp. 176 and 129.

concrete politics. It is arguable that their analysis and their verbal rituals were as stiff, predictable and stereotyped as a Punch and Judy Show, but the outline was devastatingly clear, and their political responses were sometimes angled (however woodenly) to what was actually happening and even to what could actually be done at a given time. It was thus susceptible to criticism. The contemporary Left, if very much more amiable, is marked above all by its preference for spiritual exhibitionism. To utilise another phrase of Laing, it has given up the experience of politics in exchange for the 'politics of experience'.

The contrast between 'soft' and 'hard' left needs to be related to a further contrast between the rational Left and the irrational Left before the first approximate placing of Laing on the map of left-wing ideology is possible. In its origins the Left was both the party of humanity and the party of reason, and in Marxism its abstract rationality succeeded in locating itself within the movement of history and in what was held to be a rational understanding of that movement. Now, however, the contemporary revolutionary has largely lost confidence both in the movement of history and in the efficacy of reason. The former development is mostly gain, the latter almost entirely loss.

The contrast between the rational and the irrational Left has, of course, a long history, though the contemporary drift to irrationalism and to subjectivism is particularly strong. In the present century in Britain it is possible to trace a continuous counterpoint between rationalism and romanticism within the non-communist Left; between, that is, the argued politics and articulated policies of a Bertrand Russell and the gentle apolitical withdrawals of the *gemeinschaftlich* anarchist. What Russell proposed still retained an affinity with the attitude of the hard left in being at least a kind of politics. However much marred by the silliness of great minds, it assessed certain kinds of situation, and proposed what looked like remedies.[2]

[2] See the analysis of the political attitudes of rationalists like Russell and Kingsley Martin to the pre-war crises in my *Pacifism* (1965).

What the romantic anarchists proposed was an end to politics, a generalised condemnation of western industrial society which sometimes had religious or mystical overtones and betrayed more than a penchant for what lies behind the famous phrase 'Civilisation: its cause and cure'. Lacking either a developed sociology or an articulated politics, these anarchists tended to concentrate on the liberation of the repressed psychology produced by civilisation and its discontents, or on the achievement of that liberation through sex, art and aesthetic education. Herbert Read was one of the most attractive examples of those who lay within this band of feeling and attitude. D. H. Lawrence, the archetypal contrast to Russell, provides another exemplar. 'How beastly the bourgeois is!' But whereas in the historical dramas constructed by the hard Left the bourgeois played a definable role in the predictable mechanics of the plot, for the romantic anarchists he was simply the object of ritual cursing, an all purpose stand-in for Beelzebub.

There are, of course, innumerable varieties of romantic anarchism, and not all of it is harmless artistic alienation: irrationalism can embrace both the mystique of creation or the mystique of destruction and nihilism. It can even claim to combine both, as in the slogan 'creative vandalism'. For some people destruction must precede cleansing. There is thus a hard Left as well as a soft one among the romantic anarchists, and its pedigree can be traced not only to Bakunin, but to Durutti's Barcelona and to Sorel's *Reflections on Violence*.

Another point: mystique is not far removed from mysticism. This has meant that the romantic anarchism of the Left, particularly in its soft variant, has always included an interest in these religions with a weak component of rationalism. Roman Catholicism is an allowed option, not because it is irrationalist (clearly it is not) but on account of its symbolic richness, its partial dissociation from industrial civilisation and its margin of mystical experience. Thus Herbert Read once declared that in the last analysis he stood with Pascal and Simone Weil and not their opponents, and the very names cited indicate that Catholicism itself has never been quite certain about this particular margin. No doubt that fact provides an additional attraction for the temperamentally heterodox. But beyond Catholic mysticism there has been the attraction of experiential cults from Eastern religions, and of Zen, not to mention the various mind-expanding drugs which have simultaneously served to release weary souls from the chains of everyday technical rationality and from the bondage of industrial society.

At any rate, on the 'soft' side of romantic anarchism, where R. D. Laing is mainly to be located, subjectivism, personalism, mysticism and creativity are in, whereas positivism and rationalism are out. The predominant style is not 'honourable argument': instead it is gnomic, testamental and confessional. The following paragraphs from Laing are perhaps the quintessence of both style and attitude. The first begins with a quotation from Jules Henry:

'"If all through school the young are provoked to question the Ten Commandments, the sanctity of revealed religion, the foundations of a patriotism, the profit motive, the two-party system, monogamy, the laws of incest, and so on . . .", there would,' says Laing, 'be such creativity that society would not know where to turn.' He goes on: 'Children do not give up their innate imagination, curiosity, dreaminess easily. You have to love them to get them to do that.[3] Love is the path through permissiveness to discipline: and through discipline, only too often, to betrayal of self.'

Here is the second quotation:

'And immediate experience of, in contrast to belief or faith in, a spiritual realm of demons, spirits, powers, Dominions, Principalities, Seraphim and Cherubim, the

---

[3] Something of what Laing means by love may correspond with the situation noted by D. Cooper in *Psychiatry and Anti-Psychiatry* (1967) where a mother makes statements suggesting independence and by gestures indicates that she is afraid of any attempt to implement the suggestion. Love in this sense can destroy the loved one by pre-defining all alternatives as wrong in one way or another.

Light, is even more remote. As domains of experience become more alien to us, we need greater and greater open-mindedness even to conceive of their existence.'[4]

This is the style and the atmosphere. It is in milieux which invoke visitation by indiscriminate ecstasy that Laing's writings have their provenance, and it is in a period characterised by Aleister Crowley redivivus that they resonate.

R. D. Laing was born in 1927 in Glasgow, educated at a grammar school and at Glasgow University. The flyleaves tell us that he graduated as a doctor in 1951 and became a psychiatrist in the Army for two years. He then held various posts at Glasgow Royal Mental Hospital, at the Department of Psychological Medicine at Glasgow University and the Tavistock Clinic (1957–61). He worked for the Tavistock Institute of Human Relations and has been Director first of the Langham Clinic and then of the Kingsley Hall Clinic in London since 1962. At the Tavistock Institute he concentrated initially on research on schizophrenia and the family. From 1961 to 1963 he held a fellowship of the Foundations Fund for Research in Psychiatry. So much for mere external biography.

The main writings of Laing are *The Divided Self* (1960), *The Self and Others* (1961, revised edition 1969) and *The Politics of Experience* (1967), which consists largely of miscellaneous writings from the years 1964–7. He collaborated with his fellow psychiatrist David Cooper in *Reason and Violence* (1964) which examines Sartre's principal writings between 1950 and 1960. He also collaborated with Aaron Esterson in *Sanity, Madness and the Family*, Vol. I, *The Families of Schizophrenics* (1964) and with H. Phillipson and A. R. Lee in *Interpersonal Perception* (1966). Both Laing and David Cooper helped to organise the Congress on the Dialectics of Liberation, at the Round House, Chalk Farm, in 1967, an event which resulted in twenty-three gramophone records and a book of the same name edited by Cooper. Laing contributed

---

[4] *The Politics of Experience* (1967), p. 60.

to those records and that book a piece entitled 'The Obvious', and the Introduction by Cooper illustrates how closely linked their thinking is.[5]

A broad although ultimately unreal distinction needs to be made between Laing's work as a psychiatrist, which seems to be best represented in *The Divided Self*, and his politics. It is not a prime concern of the present essay to evaluate his psychiatric work, except insofar as the leading ideas of the psychiatric school he represents are connected with his political attitudes and also insofar as the professional perspectives deriving from psychiatric training of whatever school often seem to lead to sociological and political naïveté. Clearly a discussion of this latter could develop into a full-scale sociological critique of psychiatric perspectives on social processes which is not appropriate here but which is clearly much required. All that can be attempted here is a brief summary of Laing's methodological prescriptions, and some indication of his major substantive ideas as a psychiatrist. That done, we may pass to an analysis of the broad syndrome of attitudes, and especially religious elements, embodied in Laing's work, notably as illustrated in *The Politics of Experience*.

The main methodological prescriptions of Laing are broadly of a kind with which the present writer is in sympathy. These are mostly and perhaps appropriately addressed to psychoanalysts rather than to social scientists, and are not so much new in psychoanalysis as inadequately disseminated among the general public interested in such issues. One thinker who illustrates these trends is Binswanger,[6] and he is only one of a number of theorists to whom Laing is indebted. By methodological prescriptions is meant not so much therapeutic techniques as the fundamental therapeutic strategy and personal stance taken up by the analyst in consequence of his basic assumptions about the nature of the human

[5] Cf. D. Cooper, *Psychiatry and Anti-Psychiatry* (1967).

[6] Cf. D. Cargello, *From Psychoanalytic Naturalism to Phenomenological Anthropology* (Daseinsanalyse). 'From Freud to Binswanger', in *The Human Context*, Vol. 1, No. 1, August 1968.

entity and about the status of the notion of 'person'. However, this will clearly have its impact on what one considers therapeutically and *ethically* appropriate techniques.

Perhaps Laing's position is best summarised in his own remark that one does not *have* schizophrenia, in the same way as one has the measles, one *is* schizophrenic. A succinct statement of his position is to be found on pp. 25–6 of the Introduction to *Reason and Violence*, in some paragraphs where he is discussing both Sartre's position and his own on the limits of psychoanalysis. Laing argues that at a certain point in the process of explanation some psychoanalysts cease to make their observations within the context of mutual exchange between persons and assume a one-sided superiority of objective external judgment towards the condition of the patient as if he were a mere biological organism. Both the personal relationship and 'the person' disappear.

There are several different points encapsulated here, and some confusion. For example, there is no necessary relation between stepping into an objective role for the purpose of 'judgment' and losing the reciprocity of a relationship. Indeed, there must be *some* assumption of superiority which the analyst will take up in his role as specialist in psychological dynamics, otherwise he is simply interacting with the other person. This need not be the almost absolute assumption characteristically made (say) by a consultant in relation to biological disease, since the patient is always himself experienced in what it is to be a human and often acquires insight comparable in kind if not usually in degree to that possessed by the analyst. The patient may even, in particular instances and in relation to particular aspects, have superior insight.

Presumably Laing is not objecting to the assumption that on the average and at the margin the psychoanalyst is more experienced and in a sense more objective than the patient, and therefore must on occasion step back for a 'review' on the basis of that experience, objectivity and detachment. Moreover, a doctor may recognise how marginal the superiority of his experience and how frail and partial his objectivity while not wanting to trumpet the fact to patients who are often specialists in using such admissions as means of avoiding whatever fragments of the truth the analyst has managed to acquire. He may also legitimately restrict the degree of reciprocity and involvement which he allows himself, since he, too, has to survive.

Yet there are real dangers here to which Laing points, though it is regrettable that some of his criticisms are not more specific. For example, the psychoanalytic profession is not only expert at the game of 'tails I win, heads you lose', not only curiously indifferent to external fact such as perfectly genuine threats and difficulties, not only often oblivious to ongoing social situations, but also protects itself far more than mere personal or professional survival requires in terms of a group of ploys designed to cover the extent of professional failure. These ploys are not anything very much to do with treating people as things or with biological reductionism or anything so grandiosely perverse, but are simply the verbal mechanisms for coping practically with patients, for the reduction of proliferating involvements and for the safeguarding of medical prestige. In a way one feels that Laing prefers to concentrate on the grandiose perversity to the neglect of these unhappy mundane truths. Perhaps the exploration of the personal and professional defects which psychoanalysts share with the rest of us has less éclat than accusing them of misconceived ontology, and of treating persons as things.

Just as there is no necessary relation between elements of objectivity assumed for purposes of review and the loss of genuine reciprocity, so there is no necessary connection between either of these things and treating persons as biological entities, although there may be a necessary connection in reverse, insofar as those with a biologically and neurologically reductionist approach must find it difficult to achieve a full recognition of the equality involved in person-to-person relationships. Insofar as psychoanalysts do take up biological reductionism, Laing is surely right in pointing out that it explains all and explains nothing:

'It explains all in the sense that . . . ultimately perfected biochemical and neuro-physiological techniques, and carefully delineated instinctive units of behaviour, will account "correlatively" for every possible "psychic drive" that can be thought up. Meanwhile the person, his purposes and choices (his "project") have disappeared: his ongoing mental life has been explained out, stultified with "fetishised pseudo-irreducibles".'

As Laing says, 'It is only through the discovery of a freedom, a choice of self-functioning in the face of all determinations, conditioning, fatedness, that we can attain the comprehension of a person in his full reality.'

All that is well said, though those of us who are not doctors or psychoanalysts can only wonder that those who are should discover so painfully what the rest of us are not tempted to forget: that people are, after all, people. Most human beings do not require to be reassured that a person is a person by a long détour through the more verbose, pretentious and obscure German philosophers in the existentialist and phenomenological tradition. Maybe such trials are reserved as necessities for those who specialise in the science of persons, since they, it seems, have a special facility (not to say training) in forgetting what the rest of humanity remembers without thinking about it. Yet no doubt we *do* need to think about these matters: to establish as part of a carefully articulated phenomenology and ontology the validity of personal life qua personal life, independent of our unreflective awareness of it or as imparted to us through the partly unspoken assumptions of humanist and religious traditions. A philosophical détour which articulates what one always knew is not a waste of time, and the emphasis achieved by Laing in so doing is important.

Yet it *is* an emphasis, and at times so emphatic and careless as to be absurd. Presumably what he is saying amounts to an assertion that the interpenetration of levels of analysis from physics and chemistry to existential philosophy does not destroy the independent validity of each level in its own terms or render them reducible to each other. Presumably he is also saying that reductionist assumptions lurking in the medical mind lead doctors to resort more frequently than is appropriate to drugs and to physicalist methods of dealing with particular problems, such as pre-frontal surgery and electric treatment. Occasionally he bothers to state this position in a qualified and commonsense form,[7] but at other times the assault on his own profession must seem so extreme as to prevent fellow-doctors hearing what he has to say. Thus: 'Doctors in all ages have made fortunes by killing their patients by means of their cures. The difference in psychiatry is that it is the death of the soul' (*The Dialectics of Liberation*, p. 19).

Laing's second main point with respect to methodological prescription concerns the relevance of the social context in interpreting individual psychology. This leads in two different directions: one is to establish the relevance of social context in any explanatory model of behaviour and the other involves a philosophical issue insofar as the positivistic abdication from value judgments prevents one seeing how the psychoanalyst is in his whole mode of operation expressing and executing the values of society. The latter point is linked with the issue already mentioned in relation to physicalist methods: an executioner dealing with crime by the rope does not absolve himself by declaring that ethical judgments are not his business. But the analogy is very partial, and in any case methods do not need to be physicalist for the essential point to be made that the psychoanalyst may act as an agent of current values by defining madness within the terms set by his society, thus failing to observe the partial responsibility of the mechanisms and institutions approved by that society for the genesis of mental disorder, overlooking the valid protest lurking behind the supposed abnormality,

---

[7] *The Divided Self* (1965), pp. 22–3. 'I am not here objecting to the use of mechanical or biological analogies as such, nor indeed to the intentional act of seeing man as a complex machine or animal. My thesis is limited to the contention that the theory of man as person loses its way if it falls into an account of man as a machine or man as an organismic system of processes.'

and assisting the patient to acquiesce again in the mad routines of supposedly normal people. This is an important point, however much overstated.[8]

The point about the relevance of the social context is also genuinely helpful, but it suffers like almost all psychiatric excursions into sociology from excessive universalism. Let us take Laing's wholly acceptable remark about men qua men ultimately being free, choosing as well as 'chosen'. He both asserts this as a universal truth about the human person as such and refers to the nature of capitalist society as being a near-universal social context in which that freedom is deformed. Unless he appeals to contemporary communist society as *not* implicated in such deformations, which seems an unlikely and certainly an unpersuasive recourse, he is saying that developed society as such is a universal context within which freedom is distorted. Indeed, where he appeals to an alternative type of society he actually looks back to periods notorious for their deformation of the possibility of freedom, actually postulating in one instance a decline over the past thousand years. Since he firmly indicates no concrete milieu where deformations do *not* occur, one suspects that his category of society is not limited at all, even when it appears to have special reference to capitalist society: it is society *tout court* in all its historical manifestations hitherto which is at fault. *Vide* Freud. Thus we have two universals, the universality of freedom and the universal repressiveness of society as such.

Now it is worth asking here whether men are more or less free according to the *variations* in their social milieu, within societies as well as between them. It has been suggested, for example, that the British working class is a less 'free' milieu than the middle class because it lacks the dramaturgical skills and appropriate 'role distance' (in Goffman's sense) to exercise its freedom. Without endorsing so gross a contrast it

---

[8] Occasionally even the overstatement is avoided, e.g. on pp. 90–1 of *The Politics of Experience* where he suggests his main purpose is to *loosen* any assumption that the psychiatrist is right and the patient wrong.

remains true, surely, that given milieux (within the overall repressiveness of society as conceived by Laing) do make freedom more or less accessible, so that the experience of a person in the one milieu may lead him or her to have that margin of desire to exercise freedom and therefore climb by beneficent spirals out of a psychological cul-de-sac. Conversely another person may lack just that margin and by parallel vicious spirals reach a point where he is literally without option – where he may say, quite correctly, there is no way out.

Such examples do indicate both the relevance of a milieu *much* more specific and particular than society as such (though clearly this plays its part too as an overall environment) and also the possibility of losing one's freedom, in some cases entering a vicious spiral very early in the process of life such that no human mercy or grace can save one or elicit one's free choice. Personally, I would agree with Laing that freedom is a universal option of humanity, but I would also want to know whether that affirmation, as stated by Laing, takes adequate account of the variation in its availability. At what levels of analysis is it universal, at what levels variable?

There is a subsidiary point which arises here and has some relevance to Laing's politics insofar as those people who are burdened with a metaphysic of freedom frequently ignore or despise the concrete variations in the institutionalisation of liberties. Just as a psychiatrist may proceed with a crude dichotomy of the individual and society which ignores the variable intermediate institutional network from society to society, so philosophers in the pursuit of genuine individual freedom despise the variations in stabilised liberties. British society, no doubt through a concatenation of favourable circumstances, has been relatively successful in the institutionalisation of liberties, yet Laing's criticisms presumably apply to it with equal vigour as to anywhere else, and, since he lives here, with added emotional violence. In short, the denunciatory style of radical psychiatrists touched by existential philosophy is likely to be indiscriminately global, whereas there are, after all, seven circles both in hell and in heaven.

The points just made have been related to the variable cultural context of personal freedom and of institutionalised liberty, but they also can relate to Laing's general attempt to bring the social context into account as contributing to explanation of psychological phenomena. Laing does, of course, speak of the socialisation provided by the family, and very occasionally by the school, as agents of the general socialising process emanating from global society. But he gives almost no impression whatever of the hierarchy of status and class, the processes of aspiration, of mobility and peer-group formation, and all the vastly differentiated milieux in terms of cultural pattern from one area to another, town and country, north and south. He may describe very well a highly generalised social process such as the mechanisms of gossip and scandal by which everybody is caught up in a situation which thereby acquires its own autonomous momentum because each person is primarily concerned about what the other thinks. But while he refers to persons and to groups and to society, there is little particularised social and historical location[9] through which the universal processes have to be channelled if they are to be truly explanatory.

This is perhaps more a complaint about psychiatry as such than about Laing, but it does indicate why the jeremiads and lamentations in which he engages refer so much and so indiscriminately to '*the* society', '*the* family', '*the* school' and so on. Since he seems not personally to have rejected the family, this suggests that some families in certain circumstances are better than others. The question is: which? By always referring to institutions in general, his work is a triumph of masterful evasion.

Moreover, the generality of his work also weakens his remarks about sociology, in that sociology simultaneously aspires to adequate generality and adequate particularisation. Laing's concentration on *the* group or on *the* society leads him to draw conclusions either from reading the social psychology of groups or from very abstract considerations of *the* nature of

[9] Cf. some comments by D. Cooper in *Reason and Violence* (1964), pp. 44, *et seq.*, on 'hierarchies of mediations'.

society. His comments on sociology contain very occasional slanting references to Parsons and Durkheim, but any serious acquaintance with the vast literature on the explanation of all the varied institutional patterns of modern society, or for that matter with the equally enormous literature discussing what are among his major interests – objectivity, internal personal knowledge, etc. – seem entirely lacking. While he rightly criticises Sartre for attacking sociology on the basis of fragments from Lewin (a social psychologist) and Kardiner (a 'cultural' psychoanalyst), Laing is engaged in precisely the same exercise himself.[10]

This is equally evident in his plea for an evaluative stance and an enveloping 'total' perspective within which social science may operate. Such a plea rests on an objection to positivism, the very word 'positivism' (or 'vulgar positivism') being a 'boo-word' in certain circles. The core of this objection has already been stated above insofar as it relates to the abdication of the social scientist from judgments of value and his silent implication in a supposed consensus. This is a persistent theme to which one may return later. But first let us analyse, by way of example, the statement, 'Much social science deepens the mystification. Violence cannot be seen through the sights of positivism' (*Politics of Experience*, p. 51). This issue has been discussed in a thousand academic articles, and the proportion of social scientists accepting a crude positivism is very small, whether in denying the relevance of what Polanyi calls 'personal knowledge' or in asserting an unqualified scientific objectivity, whether in dismissing value judgment as merely emotive or in refusing to acknowledge the imperatives that should operate on the scientist qua person as distinct from the special role taken up with respect to problems at a given analytic level. Sociologists are simply determined to assert that it is important at least to note the *distinction* between 'is' and 'ought'. Ethical judgments will be none the less forceful for not being confused with scientific propositions. And similarly scientific

[10] D. Cooper and R. Laing, *Reason and Violence* (1964), p. 22.

propositions will not gain by being worked up and then stuffed as a mediate element in some totalising synthesis, even one continuously constituted and reconstituted.[11] It is one of the major achievements of social science to loose itself from the bonds of ethical judgments and global metaphysics, *not* in order to reject the importance of ethics or metaphysics but to acquire a necessary (not merely a provisional) autonomy, a fragile but genuine independence for its own particular scientific purposes.

Having discussed certain aspects of Laing's methodological prescriptions one may very briefly note what are his substantive ideas in the field of psychiatry. Indeed, since a great deal of Laing's work has been on schizophrenia, it may be worthwhile utilising a summary indicating his approach from *The Divided Self*, pp. 161–4. This is perhaps the place to say that his analyses of interpersonal relations, either dyadic ones such as those between husband and wife or within the overall nexus of the family,[12] strike me as rich in insight. Such skill in understanding interpersonal relations does not of course validate his contentions vis-à-vis the geneticist-constitutional school with respect to schizophrenia, except insofar as he may quite rightly insist on the provisional hypothetical character of their approach, nor does such skill validate the naïve set of attitudes informing his political comment.

In schizophrenia the self is 'out of the body' and both wishes and fears to be reintegrated with it. The result is a disembodied self which may be lost in fantasy or engaged in a kind of dry 'observation', or else may regard itself as essentially lost or destroyed. If the self is bent on self-destruction it may do so because what has been destroyed is then eternally safe. Alternatively it may be self-destructive because it has lost any sense of the personal right to be alive, or the ability to operate with a sense of what is due to one,

[11] *Ibid.*, Part 3, Section A.
[12] As in *Interpersonal Perception* (1966).

even (say) the right to occupy a chair. The result is an experience of 'chaotic non-entity' whereby verbal expression acquires a quite bizarre and obscure coherence and in which the obscurity is deepened further because the schizophrenic is preserving his being from intrusion. His attempt at mad privacy is an effort to tell without being understood, to inform and communicate without giving anything away. To meet another person and communicate with him is to acknowledge the other's free existence and thus open up the possibility of the other treating one as a mere object. One takes no risks, because one believes that advantage will always be taken, and one may avoid any contact not only by secrecy but by an over-compliance which also expresses the sense of other people's ontological weight poised threateningly against one's own insubstantiality. Yet at the same time one's greatest desire is to be allowed to *be*, and to be understood and accepted. The schizophrenic is knocking obscurely on the walls of the sunken submarine, terrified of the dangers involved in the upward route to safety and conscious of the steady diminution of the possibility of life within.

Now in Laing's view this is a condition, or rather an experience, to be investigated not primarily on an individual basis but within a social context, notably the context of family dynamics, and these constitute a complete pattern of interaction, processes and structure. Sometimes his focus of understanding is the family, though at other times he seems to suggest that one may conceive of a kind of primary network of some twenty to thirty people within which schizophrenia is to be treated. Neither the family nor this group ought to be regarded as a pathological organism, since the problem must be viewed as an intelligible outcome of people's intentions and actions (praxis), however much the resultant processes acquire an autonomy of their own. The schizophrenic within the family and within the wider group exists to conduct its tensions, to take the brunt of its 'unlived living' and bear the weight of its crazy structure for the rest. Perhaps one might even say that 'one dies for the people' in that the rest achieve a kind of corrupt and desperate viability through the sufferings of the chosen one. In David Cooper's words, 'Most people who are called mad and who are socially victimised by virtue of that attribution ... come from family situations in which there is a desperate need to find some scapegoats, someone ... to take on the disturbance of each of the others, and, in some sense, suffer for them.'

The basic unit of interaction is dyadic, 'I' and 'You', and what happens in all the possible combinations of 'persons' in the family or beyond it can be partly illustrated in the basic interaction of personal perspectives. These constitute a kind of spiral based on how 'I' look in the view of 'the other'. As Laing puts it, this takes the form of 'I like you; you like me but I do not know that you like me; however I do know that you know I like you; and I do not know that you do know that I do not know that you like me'. This does not necessarily lead to withdrawals, but it is clearly potent with 'mismatched interpretations, expectancies, attributions and counter-attributions'[13] and is particularly relevant to understanding the various circles of misunderstanding, desolation, fear and corrosion into which husband and wife relations frequently fall.[14]

These are, if you like, the basic notions: schizophrenia as a problem of personal ontology and threats to the affirmation of personal being; the 'mad' person as essentially 'bearing' the condition of the group; and the 'spiral' of potential misunderstanding informing all interlocking personal relations, but most dramatically of all perhaps, the dyad of husband and wife.

Such a brief account, however inadequate, does allow us to move on to an analysis of the underlying personal attitudes of Laing, since the fact that he sets a particular type of 'abnormal' experience within a social context, coupled with a suspicion of the psychiatrist as representing an undesirable society, allows him to question both the abnormality of the

[13] *Interpersonal Perception* (1966), pp. 21 and 38.
[14] Cf. R. D. Laing, H. Phillipson and A. R. Lee, 'The Spiral of Perspectives', *New Society*; November 10, 1966.

supposedly mentally ill and the normality of the society which is the context of the illness. Indeed it is perhaps central to Laing's position that modern society attempts to turn every child into a conformist and in so doing deprives the child of its potentialities and creativity, devastating its being with the chains we choose to call love. The child has gradually to be converted to a treason against itself by making a pact with the madness of society. And in this process the schizophrenic may be the one who cannot suppress his instincts enough to perform the much-solicited treason. The psychiatrist is not so much the objective representative of health as the corrupt solicitor, the secret agent of society whose modus operandi is tainted by precisely the ills he attempts to heal. (Those who do not view patients as persons depersonalise themselves.)

Here one must turn to a group of ideas and attitudes which provide a bridge passage between his psychiatric stance and his politics: they are contained in the notion of the 'mystification of violence'. For Laing, a central element in the broader task of 'demystification' is an attempt to 'demystify' violence, and the essence of this task is to recover access to that direct experience which socialisation so successfully violates and destroys. Socialisation, for him, is the local agent of that canalised institutional violence which is located in central government and which stalks society cloaked in the language and unspoken assumptions of the mass media. Socialisation is the first and primal violence against the person which can only be met by projecting violence on to others, acting violently towards them and justifying oneself by attributing violence to them. *It is this view of socialisation which links the experience of the family to politics, psychiatry to global issues, approaches to upbringing and pedagogical method to Vietnam.*

For people of this mind, all delimitation of issues, all academic division of scholarly labour, and all attempts to view phenomena objectively from a variety of specialised perspectives at different analytic levels, are part of a policy of divide in order to rule. There can be no taking apart of Humpty-Dumpty even in order to put him together again: the question is, as Humpty-Dumpty himself said, 'Who is master?' The appeal of this to the kind of young person looking for quick global answers, impatient with the requirements of careful study, and armed with a drifting paranoid suspicion of all authority, is obvious. The psychology of identifying a malevolent 'Them', which he describes, is unusually well developed in his followers.

Global accusation, like libel and rumour, is easy: refutation, like art, is long and difficult. There is no answer to a grain of truth eked out by indiscriminate misrepresentation except a disciplined understanding. It would take too long; but one can at least begin by pointing to the central assumption, derived from Rousseau, that man as man is originally innocent, and civilisation, especially modern civilisation, the focus of original sin. Incidentally, it is interesting that this assumption links Laing with another large success in the field of commercial publishing: the type of egregious ethological speculation represented by *The Human Zoo* and *The Naked Ape*. In short there are those who see human institutions as dykes canalising a raw, variable, morally ambiguous human potential into the fructifying ways of civilisation, and those who see those institutions as barriers to a flood of inherent generosity, innate humanity and abounding creativity. Laing is of the latter.

That said, it is instructive to look more closely at what appears to be a very confused discussion (pp. 50–3 of *The Politics of Experience*) which Laing conducts concerning socialisation, violence and value judgments. What he says is this. First, socialisation, including moral and political socialisation, is a violence against personal experience because it is socially derived and imposed rather than individually achieved. Now it is not clear how else moral perspectives can be derived in the first instance except from society, and it is even less clear that people do not, as they mature, partly transform what is so derived into a personal and critical perspective. Secondly, Laing argues that to regard animals and humans in a given scientific context as (e.g.) biochemical complexes is equivalent to a denial of their true nature as animals and persons; and such a context prevents those who adopt it from an ethical response when violence against men and animals is perpetrated.

Now there is a tiny grain of truth here, which is that a person specialising at a given level of scientific interest such as biochemistry may become so professionally deformed as to forget that what he studies is also a human being, may indeed refuse to acknowledge that in principle results may need to be reassimilated within a wider view which includes the specifically human. Humpty-Dumpty may lie shattered on the floor. It may even happen that such an attitude enters into a scientist's general moral perspective. But it happens to a certain degree to certain people, and the extent to which it does would require extensive documentation; unfortunately the techniques of the propagandist asserting the primacy of his 'genuine' human experience do not allow so wasteful an expenditure of intellectual energy in the cause of mere verification. It is more economical and more effective to say, 'Meanwhile Vietnam goes on.' And here, of course, one encounters a cheapness of effect which in Laing goes with this kind of intellectual economising. The situation in Vietnam is too appalling, the issues too confused, the murderous intent on both sides too typical of war at almost all times, for it to be used as a catch-all riposte by those too lazy or too frenetic to engage in honourable argument.

In any case, a more appropriate intellectual economy might have been employed, since what is being said is even more simple than appears. Laing is claiming that his value judgments are rooted in his genuine experience as a human being, whereas those who disagree with him are the deluded facsimiles of over-successful socialisation. He has not adequately considered the possibility that – to quote him from a different context – his opponents may be people like himself, dressed differently. They, too, may be human.

With world enough and time, it would be worth while indicating just how grossly Laing exaggerates the pressure of socialisation on the child in the democratic West as compared with almost any other period or type of society. It is in fact so affected by a degree of indecision and by a measure of self-indulgent irresponsibility (backed by fashionable psychologies) about its right to socialise, that it often neglects to give those firm, compassionate guidelines within the family and the school without which the child is a flailing ego. Many children rightly suspect that absence of discipline is absence of love. Our school systems are attempting to achieve a balance between required structures and individuality: if they err it is sometimes in taking the sentimentalities deriving from Rousseau too seriously, in acceding too easily to callow cults of spontaneity. On the contrary, it is the duty of a home or school proudly and exultantly to induct a child into that incredibly rich human achievement called civilisation, and into those social, spiritual and intellectual disciplines on which it is built.

It would also be worth showing that some element of mystification is inherent in every civilised social achievement, including the violence socialised, rationalised and sometimes civilised, in the state. Masked (or 'mystified') violence is often a step forward in a peaceable direction; in certain circumstances men gradually conform to their own peaceful self-portraits and are pressed by opinion to implement their misleading idealisations. Men always partially misrepresent their actions: legitimate and minimum authority can be labelled repressive violence; repression can be labelled the maintenance of civilised order. That is not surprising. Men do attempt to delude themselves and others. There are indeed certain situations where the total truth is the grossest violence and where the question is always: what is the most responsible and compassionate proportion of truth and delusion? That is as true of politics as it is of person-to-person relations. Confronted by one's own humanity and others', there is only one possibility: a relaxed compassion towards oneself and other people.

The logic of Laing's position is ultimately violent and totalitarian in spite of (or because of) its extreme libertarian gloss. Perhaps its possibilities are best illustrated by a passage from John Gerassi in *The Dialectics of Liberation* (p. 93). Gerassi presents as an alternative to Stalinism something exemplified in Cuba, where 'one way to guarantee that their people are genuinely free is not elections, is not free press, is not all the trappings of the so-called political democracy that we have, but simply to arm their people'. In short, if democracy and a free press are less genuine than they claim, the best answer is to abolish free elections and ban open comment; and the best response to militaristic tendencies is the total militarisation of everybody. It is a curious consummation to the metaphysics of freedom.

This is the framework, these the plausible half and quarter-truths which are major keys to the syndrome of attitudes found in Laing. They are allied to a stress on the need for transcendence, which is in part a range of experience akin to mystical illumination which modern society is held to inhibit and denigrate and which is also an ability to see beyond the confines of one-dimensionality to another mode of social life. Since this is important, any exposition must include some reference to the religious elements found in Laing: our alienation from ecstasy and the problem of an original sin uniquely focused in capitalist society. The best way into such an exposition is to concentrate on these attitudes as illustrated in *The Politics of Experience*, and to preface them with a brief look at Laing's contribution to *The Dialectics of Liberation* entitled, *The Obvious*. The crucial point for criticism of Laing is the contrast between his politics of experience and the experience of politics.

It is 'obvious' to Laing that what is 'irrational' in the individual can be understood in the context of the family, and that the irrationality of the family is intelligible within its 'encompassing networks', and so on up to the society itself and the total social world system. Each of the wider systems pervades the smaller sub-systems. There is nothing within which the irrationality of the world may be made intelligible, unless it be God, and perhaps He is mad too. Social salvation is not possible by individual conversion nor by seizing the state apparatus but by working outwards from the middle range of institutions, e.g. factories and schools. Psychiatry is the unwitting agent of a political operation against the individual, and the patients are thrown up and selected by a system of which psychiatrists are the malign solicitors. This violence against the individual is paralleled by violence on the societal scale: while the micro-system selects an individual, the macro-system selects 'them'. 'Them' currently comprise the Third World, the have-nots, the exploited. We are enabled to see the Third World as 'them' by our own misconception of what we wrongly believe to be the western desire for peace and by our faith in its vaunted democracy. We project our own unjust violence on to them, are surprised at their just violence against us, and so feel justified in destroying Vietnam.

So universal is our ignorance of and obedience to this system that the number of those surviving as human beings is minute. Socialisation makes us into unwitting subjects of the system just as psychiatrists are made into its unwitting agents. The normal mode of socialisation, terrorisation into submission by love, repeats an endless spiral back through countless generations to the beginning. This spiral backwards is the precondition of our projecting a world composed of 'us' and 'them' in which the hatefulness of 'them' is ourselves seen in the mirror. The crux of the system is obedience resting on the generation of guilt and on the reflex of believing in the authorities. The state, the church, the government, scholarship and science – authority and authorities – all are partners in such a morass of delusion that almost nothing can be truly known: we can only trust something deeper than ourselves, and it is most obvious that *this* is most hidden.

These basic themes are simply found on a larger scale in *The Politics of Experience*: white western society, its governmental system, its methods of upbringing, its science and its scholarship are part of a tissue of delusion which is responsible for stereotyped divisions into 'us' and 'them', and is to blame for violence and counterviolence. We think 'they' are to blame; not at all, it is we who are to blame in the world. This is a simple diagnosis, easily achieved by standing an equally simple diagnosis on its head. The basic stratagem of this style of thinking is: if you want to know what to believe, find out what is the current consensus and turn it upside down; that way you won't necessarily be right but at least you won't inevitably be wrong. If, in addition, you hope for a hint as to what is right, listen to those whom society stigmatises as abnormal. They've got something.

As one proceeds to document the Laingian position one can hardly help noticing two characteristics in his own work which illustrate his own analysis of what constitutes a fundamentally irrational view of the world. One is the simple stereotyping of 'us' and 'them', encapsulated in vast assertions about what people in western societies think: a grandiose simplification of all issues achieved by stigmatising whole societies as solidary elements in 'the Enemy'. No evidence is cited, just projections about what people in the disapproved societies are projecting about 'them'. This looks like an unfortunate example of the spiral perspectives in which Laing is himself a specialist. The other characteristic is the repetition on the macro-scale of what he describes as inherent in the experience of schizophrenia on the micro-scale. All other types of society *except* his own have some kind of ontological root, something which may be admired, some kind of right to exist. Only that which is his own constitutes a kind of delusion, a mass of subhumanity, suffering from ontological weightlessness. There is in Laing's writing not a single word suggesting that any virtue inheres in what is his own inheritance. So total a rejection, so wholehearted a separating out of the self from the body of society, so extraordinary a fear of becoming re-attached to it by fiendish subtleties, looks like a curious analogue of the self hating what is most truly its own.[15] Perhaps the condition could be called macro-schizophrenia.

In *The Politics of Experience* the viewpoint expressed is religious not only in the chapter concerned with 'transcendental experience' but throughout. The word religious is not used figuratively: it happens to be accurate. The more extreme forms of a religious rejection of the world often result in two apparently contradictory responses both illustrated in Laing: the first is a flailing violence towards all mundane

[15] David Holbrook's criticism of Laing – 'Madness to Blame Society' (*Twentieth Century*, 2, 1969) – points to the seductive charm of blaming

structures, all those things which for others may mediate elements of truth and personal being. Roles, institutions and everyday experience are rejected because what they mediate is not *the* Truth, because they partly mask what they partly reveal. This obsessive pilgrimage towards the Absolute may result in a total rejection of all the way-stations where other people have rested on their journey, and in an excoriating contempt for their blindness. They are the blind led by the blind. They 'scurry into roles, statuses, identities, inter-personal relations'. In other words they escape into the bolt-holes of partial sanity because they cannot bear too much sanity, just as others escape into partial madness because they have an inkling how partial the sanity found in those boltholes really is. Laing's choice of visionary viewpoint is allied to Eliot's 'Mankind cannot bear very much reality', but without his compassion.

The second form taken by this religious rejection of the world is silence, because the search for the Absolute has been attempted and failed. The Truth itself was not available (or only intermittently) and, since all the mediate intervening half-truths have been rejected, nothing can be said. Speech is an impropriety and the structured or prepared speech is a blasphemous attempt at order when no order is possible. This is close to the Quaker experience. One must be silent concerning that which cannot be spoken. As Laing puts it, 'Black on the canvas, silence on the screen, an empty white sheet of paper, are perhaps feasible. There is little con-

---

'society' for everything. He also suggests that in treating schizophrenia the analyst can come to play out for himself the meanings he desperately attributes to the patient. A histrionic manner is acquired which the analyst finds increasingly real to him until he feels lost outside schizophrenic company. To get through to the patient he adopts an exaggerated pose as a fellow-sufferer which requires him to blow up the oppressiveness of social situations and act contemptuously to ordinary common life and the normal sources of identity. Having originally seen the patient as an oracle, the analyst becomes oracular. Holbrook himself describes this as an essential self-indulgence according well with the attitude 'I'm this way because society . . ., etc., etc.' Naturally this attitude is in some tension with assertions of existential freedom. Cf. also P. Sedgwick 'Laing's clangs' (*New Society*, January 14, 1970).

junction of truth and social "reality".' Stylistically the only mode of expression is unprepared, unstructured, gnomic, enigmatic. There is no truth in mere knowledge, no truth in social forms, no truth in ourselves. 'We are all murderers and prostitutes. . . .' Here the Quaker experience mutates back to the characteristic Calvinist experience: the total reprobation in which man as man is universally implicated. Indeed, in Laing we have constant shifts between four main modes of the religious consciousness: mystical experience of the *coincidentia oppositorum*, intense prophetic violence, withdrawal into silence, into institutional and intellectual dissolution, and total reprobation. And Laing himself, through a residual Presbyterianism, is unwilling to assert that he is one of the Elect – 'the survivors'. As he puts it: 'We who are half alive, living in the often fibrillating heartland of a senescent capitalism. . . . Can we do more than sing our sad and bitter songs of disillusion and defeat?' *Super flumina Babylonis* . . . the reference appears to be to capitalism *or* to Babylon: universalised it is the essence of the religious awareness that 'here we have no abiding city'. Whether our civilisation is so hostile to this awareness as he maintains, so relentlessly secular, as compared with others, is open to doubt. The nature of the dissent it is capable of producing may be taken both as its condemnation and its salvation. Laing himself contradicts his own thesis. It is a kind of compliment.

Although religious experience can achieve a general prophetic denunciation of a given social condition it is a poor guide to day-to-day politics. These are inevitably, and *quite properly*, conducted in a dubious half-light of more or less unhappy compromises, and to the extent that they are invaded by religion then either each shifty pragmatic compromise is papered over by religious legitimation or intimations of the New Jerusalem drive *l'homme moyen sensuel* relentlessly and intolerantly towards a predestined goal. Essentially the politics of experience are no adequate guide to the experience of politics; a denunciation is not a viable policy. It is this fact that should be the basis of any critical appraisal of the type of politico-religious awareness found in Laing.

When earlier in this essay I located Ronald Laing on the fringes of the irrationalist Left there was one sense perhaps in which it was untrue. He does not explicitly embrace irrationalism, and indeed he uses the word 'irrational' to stigmatise institutions and activities of which he disapproves. However, in such instances he rarely tells us what he means by 'irrational' and one can only assume he uses the word simply as a stand-in for emotional disapproval. He can certainly be considered an irrationalist in that he finds rational and argued discussion of religious questions uncongenial, and insists that the essence of religion is ecstasy. And while it would be better to regard ecstasy as supra-rational rather than irrational, there is in Laing's whole style a *substitution* of ecstasy for argument and a disinclination to build up a sequence of ordered points, supported by carefully collected evidence, qualified in respect of this issue or that.

His method consists in random accusation and sloganised virulence, which destroys the possibility of genuine discussion. Patient refutation has to build up on a basis of carefully verified evidence, has to define its terms (whereas Laing simply prefers to use them) and eventually to build up a cumulative impression, usually in terms of more or less, of marginally this rather than that. Such a method cannot compete with a rhetorical either/or, with grossly simplified alternatives, with slogans used as an excuse for not thinking. You cannot talk with a man who throws his sincerity at you and who persistently implies that you and every other person who disagrees with him is a racialist, an anti-semite and a crass authoritarian. It is like a discussion arranged between a Pentecostalist in the pulpit and a Unitarian in the congregation: the convention within which the exchange takes place is set by the enthusiast, not by the enquirer.

Laing will not engage in rational argumentation because that is not the way converts are made. Laing is also an irrationalist in the sense that he proposes no means to achieve his vision, apart from offering vague hints about psychic subversion in the middle-range type of institution, such as the school and the university. He proposes no policies, articulates no alternatives, raises no queries about viability, weighs no costs and advantages, assesses no immediate and remote consequences. For obvious reasons: if he did, the whole visionary edifice would collapse like the baseless fabric of a dream. The old Left at least proposed a method of bringing dreams to fruition: when that method proved a nightmare the Left was reduced to the dream again and to variants of peyote. Not indeed that mankind should or can give up its dreams, but without an articulated machinery for the dream to be brought on stage it remains generalised in proclamations, embedded in rituals and confined to what can be achieved by sympathy and goodwill: in short, it remains religious. Holy Communion – by sharing bread and wine – is a symbol and sometimes also a realisation of a preliminary achievement in brotherhood and a pointer to the need for extending both its fellowship and the presence at the heart of that fellowship: but it cannot substitute for the pragmatic turmoil and administrative grind and cold calculation necessary for political action. Politics cannot simply be a Gospel, or else that Gospel eventually declines not only into ritual but into mere ritual.

So much contemporary protest of the kind that Laing admires seems to consist of precisely these rituals and exhibitions executed by those who have no access to the idea of cost and are therefore unwilling to pay the administrative and personal costs of their gospels. For example, Laing's collaborator David Cooper refers to the schizophrenic as the author of the 'totally gratuitous crazy act' and the once-for-all 'happening' is precisely this: a negative symbol whose only point is its negation and which explodes violently into nothingness. As Laing himself might put it: a 'happening' is the negation of the negation. On the continuum running from pragmatic articulated politics to the gratuitous crazy act Laing and Cooper stand about midway, but their sympathies clearly turn towards the latter end of that continuum. They find it easy to indulge in generalised abuse of politicians, easy to sympathise with the psychotic and to regard him as less 'estranged from reality' than the politician. Yet sympathy for psychotics need not be linked to a modish contempt for politicians.

There is no more important task in defending the disciplines of civilisation against writers such as Laing than the rehabilitation of the political vocation. The abuse of politicians is one of the major forms of contemporary self-indulgence. In the demonology of those who aspire to be *real human beings* (and who so often inflict their humanity indiscriminately on others) politicians are the archetypes of the straw man, drained of all ontological root. They are regarded as the prisoners of themselves and the gaolers of the rest of us. Yet in this competition for ontological supremacy perhaps even the politicians and the bureaucrats have a chance. When one considers the nature and constraints of politics there is perhaps in politicians a kind of heroism. Let us at least nominate them as competitors in the ontological stakes, alongside those traditionally easy winners, the artists and intellectuals.

The politician can be a man who wears a mask over his humanity in order the better to serve that humanity. Admittedly it is often an orthodox conventional mask: yet it could be that behind the disguise lies more humanity than in those who affect no disguises, whose appearance of open-hearted innocence depends on the proclivity for unmasking other people. In any case, many people accept the disciplines which require a mask in a certain limited area of their life, say their profession, but are able to relax into simple humanity in every other sphere of their life; others have no imperative need for masks in any area of their lives, perhaps because they have chosen just those areas of social life where the discipline of social relations can be lax and easy, where few exigencies constrict and few responsibilities congeal. The politician, however, has chosen a role where exigency and responsibility demand a mask at nearly all times.

Consider the following proposition: that the highest moral responsibility could conceivably reside in a civil servant, or a politician at the Ministry of Defence, who uses the coolest rational calculation to tread that narrow edge which is marginally closer to survival than all the alternatives. Once such a man has chosen a policy he is within certain limits committed to it, indeed knows in advance that what he has chosen may acquire a momentum which will control him. He knows it includes certain costs, may in extreme circumstances begin to include further costs which may be appalling, but which when that stage has been reached are probably (but not certainly) less appalling than the alternative costs. Perhaps such a man is a *kind* of genuine human being: willing to accept what it will be like to live with himself and with the obloquy of those not in his shoes should the worst happen.

As the consequences of his choice accumulate he becomes totally immersed in fending off the worst, and this may mean the death of his personality; nothing but a public life and an 'insane' commitment to politics. Not even the relief of an autobiographical exposition of his motives is open to him: he can only advise and act. Whatever he does now will acquire no honour in the world of those easily achieved martyrdoms undertaken in 'progressive' causes. Indeed he may have to face the obloquy of seeming to acquiesce in and abet just such a martyrdom. This kind of man accepts the need for painful struggle and refuses to inveigh easily against the structures of reality, but instead employs the highest rational cunning to play those structures as far as they can be played: this is both a creative act of his own *and* an encounter with a strange, alien, recalcitrant otherness.

His highest achievement will be a tiny victory, his normal achievement just to survive. This he will never be able openly to explain, and may have to accept the mortification of having to claim that a tiny victory was a great one. He may even acquire a reputation among the cognoscenti for naïve reasoning and dishonest appeals, simply because the public neither wishes to know his actual reasons nor would be willing to face the stark alternatives involved in that reasoning. It may even be that he is a man of the highest intelligence who must accept the contempt of an intelligentsia which has never tried to understand why he must appear stupid in public and appear ignorant of what he may know better than anyone. Perhaps such a man has some claim to his humanity and ours.